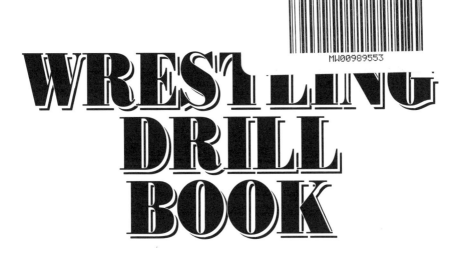

WRESTLING DRILL BOOK

Dennis A. Johnson, MS
Eisenhower High School
Warren County, PA

Leisure Press
Champaign, Illinois

Library of Congress Cataloging-in-Publication Data

Johnson, Dennis A.
    Wrestling drill book / by Dennis A. Johnson.
        p.   cm.
    Includes index.
    ISBN 0-88011-401-0
    1. Wrestling--Training. I. Title.
    GV1196.4.T7J65   1991
    796.8'12--dc20   90-38916

ISBN: 0-88011-401-0

Acquisitions Editor: Brian Holding
Developmental Editor: June I. Decker, PhD
Managing Editor: Valerie Hall
Assistant Editors: Kari Nelson, Timothy Ryan, Dawn Levy
Copyeditor: Wendy Nelson
Proofreader: Karin Leszczynski
Production Director: Ernie Noa
Typesetter: Yvonne Winsor
Text Design: Keith Blomberg
Text Layout: Tara Welsch
Cover Design: Jack Davis
Cover Photo: John Kilroy
Interior Photos: David P. Case
Interior Photo Models: Chuck Grinnen, Todd Reynolds
Printer: United Graphics

Leisure Press books are available at special discounts for bulk purchase for sales promotions, premiums, fund-raising, or educational use. Special editions or book excerpts can also be created to specification. For details, contact the Special Sales Manager at Leisure Press.

Printed in the United States of America

10 9 8 7 6 5 4 3 2 1

Leisure Press
A Division of Human Kinetics
    Publishers, Inc.
Box 5076, Champaign, IL 61825-5076
1-800-747-4457

UK Office:
Human Kinetics Publishers (UK) Ltd.
PO Box 18
Rawdon, Leeds LS19 6TG
England
(0532) 504211

In the past decade, six Sheffield Area High School wrestlers have met with tragedy during their school years or shortly after graduation.

Robbie, Gary, Marvin, Chuck, Seder, and Ozzie—"This book is for you guys."

CONTENTS

FOREWORD

Wrestling is a diverse sport with many skills, techniques, holds, and strategies. As young wrestlers, we practice our moves hundreds of times hoping to improve our technique so we can succeed in competition. Even the most experienced wrestlers use drills to perfect their wrestling techniques as they strive for excellence.

In the *Wrestling Drill Book*, Dennis Johnson has compiled drills for every level of wrestling. He has divided the book into various skill areas and includes drills for beginners through elite wrestlers. To help encourage student participation and enthusiasm, Mr. Johnson has included a chapter on games and contests.

Whether you are a coach or a wrestler, this book will help you develop wrestling skills and techniques through the use of drills. As a college coach, elite wrestler, and camp instructor, I am frequently asked about drills to help people become better wrestlers or coaches. This book has given me a new source of drills and games to share with those in the wrestling public who want to be the best they can be.

Bruce R. Baumgartner
Olympic and World Champion Wrestler
Edinboro University Assistant Wrestling Coach

PREFACE

This book has two purposes—to describe specific technique drills, warm-up drills, and wrestling-related games for the enhancement of technical wrestling development around the world, and to encourage student participation in the combative sport of wrestling. The *Wrestling Drill Book* is a vital tool for your teaching, whether you are a novice or a seasoned wrestling coach.

In the early 1980s, USA Wrestling identified seven basic skills it feels wrestlers need to become successful: position, motion, level change, penetration, backstep, lifting, and back arch. Numerous books and articles published by coaches illustrate many additional styles and techniques available to amateur wrestlers. There are technique books to cover every phase of wrestling, from the takedown to the tilt to the pin.

The focus of this book differs from most others because its drills are designed primarily to enhance performance of the seven basic skills and to lead up to specific wrestling moves. For example, before a wrestler can effectively execute a double leg takedown, he must practice changing levels and penetration.

I have illustrated many drills with photos and have described them with key phrases to help create mental images for wrestlers. Beginning coaches will find the wrestling games and activities especially useful for developing and maintaining interest among students. One of those activities (like Mat Chess or Sumo Wrestling) just might spark the career of a future Olympian.

Coaches are continually working to improve their programs to compete successfully, whether their athletes wrestle at the novice or the international level. The many drills and games compiled in this book can be used to form a solid base for fundamental skill development and to encourage participation in any wrestling program.

ACKNOWLEDGMENTS

I would like to thank all of the coaches who have cooperated in this venture by contributing drills for this book. I would like to give special thanks to John Fritz of Penn State University, Mike Gill and Gary Barton of Clearfield High School, and Rob Johnson of Shikellamy High School for their in-depth interviews.

A note of appreciation goes to photographer David P. Case and the models, Todd Reynolds and Chuck Grinnen, for their time, effort, and patience during the photo sessions. Finally, I would like to thank Christine Cataldo-Meneo for her continued support during the creation of this text. Thanks all!

DRILL CONTRIBUTORS

Arizona
Glenn McMinn   Apache Junction High School
Rick St. Clair   Apache Junction High School

Colorado
Mark Schmidt   Centaurus High School

Florida
Russ Cozart   Brandon High School

Georgia
Cliff Ramos   Meadowcreek High School

Illinois
John Jobst   John Hersey High School
Rick Mann   John Hersey High School

New York
Dean Johnson   Alfred State College

Ohio
Mickey Balmert   Bishop Ready High School
Kevin Peck   Licking Heights High School
Doug Darnell   Dublin High School
Robert Seaquist   John Alder High School
Allen Brown   New Albany High School

Pennsylvania
James Neuman   Cannon-MacMillen High School
Curtis Griffin   Waynesburg High School
Joe Ayersman   Waynesburg High School
George DeAugustino   North Allegheny Junior High School
John Fritz   Penn State University
Dan Johnson   Penn State University
Gary Barton   Clearfield High School
Mike Gill   Clearfield High School
Ron Smith   Clearfield Junior High School

Steve Rood	Cranberry High School
Mike Maines	Erie East High School
Joe Cesari	North Schuylkill High School
Rob Johnson	Shikellamy High School
Phil Lockcuff	Shikellamy High School
Joe Letko	Eisenhower High School
Lenny Ferraro	Brookville High School
Joe Schoffstall	Edinboro University
Pat Pecora	University of Pittsburgh at Johnstown
Carlton Haselrig	University of Pittsburgh at Johnstown
Tony Fera	Youngsville High School
David Cataldo	Warren High School
James Miller	Sheffield High School

Virginia

Jim Manchester	Spotsylvania High School

West Virginia

John Hawley	Charleston High School
Phil Oldham	Parkersburg South High School
Bill Archer	Huntington High School
Dr. C. Robert Barnett	Marshall University
Dean Sanders	Marshall University

DRILL FINDER

Neutral Position Wrestling Drills

OFFENSE

Ankle pick or sweep 1.30, 1.31, 1.32, 1.33, 1.34, 3.11, 3.12, 4.12

Back arch 1.34, 2.1, 2.7, 2.8, 2.9, 2.10, 2.11, 2.12, 2.13, 3.12, 3.13

Arm drag 1.34, 3.5, 3.6, 3.7, 3.11, 3.12, 3.13

Backstep 1.34, 2.5, 2.6, 2.10, 2.11, 2.12, 3.12, 3.13

Bodylock 1.34, 2.3, 2.11, 2.12, 3.12, 3.13, 4.12

Double leg 1.12, 1.16, 1.17, 1.26, 1.34, 3.8, 3.10, 3.11, 3.12, 3.13, 8.4

Duckunder 1.34, 2.1, 2.12, 3.1, 3.2, 3.3, 3.4, 3.11, 3.12, 3.13

Fireman's 3.11, 3.12, 3.13

Headlock 1.34, 2.3, 2.11, 2.12, 3.12, 3.13, 4.12

Hip toss 1.34, 2.10, 2.11, 2.12, 3.12

Level change 1.5, 1.7, 1.8, 1.9, 1.10, 1.11, 1.12, 1.13, 1.14, 1.15, 1.16, 1.17, 1.18, 1.19, 1.20, 1.21, 1.22, 1.23, 1.24, 1.25, 1.26, 1.27, 1.28, 1.29, 1.30, 1.31, 1.32, 1.33, 1.34, 2.4, 2.12, 3.2, 3.3, 3.4, 3.5, 3.6, 3.7, 3.8, 3.9, 3.10, 3.11, 3.12, 3.13, 4.12

Lifting 1.22, 1.34, 2.1, 2.4, 2.11, 2.12, 2.13, 3.12, 4.12

Motion 1.3, 1.4, 1.5, 1.6, 1.7, 1.8, 1.9, 1.10, 1.11, 1.12, 1.13, 1.14, 1.15, 1.16, 1.17, 1.18, 1.19, 1.20, 1.21, 1.23, 1.27, 1.28, 1.29, 1.30, 1.31, 1.32, 1.33, 1.34, 2.4, 2.12, 3.2, 3.3, 3.4, 3.5, 3.6, 3.7, 3.8, 3.9, 3.10, 3.11, 3.12, 3.13, 4.1, 4.3, 4.12

Penetration 1.11, 1.12, 1.13, 1.14, 1.15, 1.16, 1.17, 1.18, 1.19, 1.20, 1.23, 1.24, 1.25, 1.26, 1.27, 1.28, 1.29, 1.30, 1.31, 1.32, 1.33, 1.34, 2.2, 2.4, 2.12, 3.2, 3.3, 3.4, 3.5, 3.6, 3.7, 3.8, 3.9, 3.10, 3.11, 3.12, 3.13, 4.12

Position 1.1, 1.2, 1.3, 1.4, 1.5, 1.6, 1.7, 1.8, 1.9, 1.10, 1.11, 1.12, 1.13, 1.14, 1.15, 1.16, 1.17, 1.18, 1.19, 1.20, 1.23, 1.27, 1.28, 1.29,

1.30, 1.31, 1.32, 1.33, 1.34, 2.4, 2.12, 3.2, 3.3, 3.4, 3.5, 3.6, 3.7, 3.9, 3.10, 3.11, 3.12, 3.13, 4.12

Single leg 1.13, 1.18, 1.19, 1.20, 1.22, 1.23, 1.24, 1.27, 1.28, 1.29, 1.34, 2.1, 3.8, 3.10, 3.11, 3.12, 3.13, 4.12, 8.15

Takedown setups 1.34, 3.4, 3.5, 3.6, 3.7, 3.8, 3.10, 3.11, 3.12, 3.13, 8.4

DEFENSE

Butt drags 4.3, 4.9, 4.10, 4.12, 8.4

Front headlocks 1.25, 3.13, 4.7, 4.8, 4.12

Neutral position defense 4.1, 4.2, 4.3, 4.4, 4.5, 4.6, 4.7, 4.8, 4.9, 4.10, 4.11, 4.12, 4.13

Pancakes 4.6, 4.12

Snapdowns 2.4, 3.13, 4.3, 4.5, 4.12, 4.13, 5.5, 8.4

Sprawling 4.1, 4.2, 4.3, 4.4, 4.12, 4.13, 8.4

Whizzers 4.1, 4.2, 4.3, 4.11, 4.12

Referee's Position Wrestling Drills

WRESTLING SKILL	RELATED DRILL
Bridge maneuvers	6.16, 8.2, 8.3, 8.4, 8.8, 8.9
Cradles	4.12, 5.12, 5.13, 5.15, 7.12
Destroying base	5.7, 5.10, 5.11, 5.16, 5.17
Floating	5.6, 5.9, 5.12
Halfs	2.12, 5.14, 5.18
Hand control, position, and base maintenance	1.34, 5.6, 6.1, 6.2, 6.3, 6.4, 6.5, 6.6, 6.7, 6.11, 6.18, 6.26
Hip heist	6.7, 6.12, 6.13, 6.14
Legs	5.15, 5.19, 5.20, 5.21
Rolls	5.6, 5.8, 5.9, 6.19, 6.20, 6.21, 6.22
Sits	5.6, 5.9, 6.13, 6.14, 6.15, 6.16, 6.17, 6.25
Spinning	4.5, 4.12, 5.1, 5.2, 5.3, 5.4, 5.5

Standups	1.34, 5.6, 5.16, 5.17, 6.5, 6.6, 6.7, 6.8, 6.9, 6.10
Switch	5.6, 5.9, 6.23, 6.24
Tilts	2.12, 5.10

Games and Contests

TYPES	RELATED CONTESTS
Dual contests	7.2, 7.3, 7.4, 7.5, 7.6, 7.7, 7.8, 7.9, 7.10, 7.18, 7.21A, 7.22, 7.23, 7.24, 7.25, 7.26, 7.30
Escapes and reversal contests	5.4, 6.18
Hand control, position, and base maintenance contests	6.3, 6.18, 7.3, 7.8, 7.28
Physical education team games	7.11, 7.13, 7.14, 7.18, 7.19, 7.20, 7.21B, 7.27, 7.28, 7.29, 7.31
Pin drill contests	5.18, 7.12
Riding contests	5.4, 5.6, 5.8, 5.9, 5.10, 5.11, 5.16, 5.17, 5.20, 6.18, 7.1
Scramble wrestling contests	6.26, 7.4, 7.6, 7.7
Takedown contests	1.19, 1.20A, 1.32, 2.4, 4.10, 7.2, 7.3, 7.5, 7.8, 7.9, 7.13, 7.18, 7.26C
Tilting contests	5.10, 6.18, 7.15, 7.16, 7.17
Wrestling team games	7.11, 7.13, 7.14, 7.15, 7.16, 7.17, 7.18, 7.19, 7.20, 7.27, 7.28, 7.29, 7.31

Conditioning Activities

TYPE	RELATED DRILL
Arm activities	7.20, 7.22, 7.23, 8.2, 8.3, 8.4, 8.5, 8.6, 8.12
Back activities	8.2, 8.3, 8.4, 8.10, 8.12, 8.13, 8.16

Cardiovascular activity	8.1, 8.2, 8.3, 8.4
Chest activities	8.2, 8.3
Handgrip activities	8.2, 8.3, 8.5, 8.6, 8.17
Leg activities	2.1, 2.2, 7.10, 7.23, 8.2, 8.3, 8.4, 8.11
Muscle endurance activity	2.2, 7.10, 8.2, 8.3, 8.4, 8.5, 8.6, 8.7
Neck activities	7.21C, 8.2, 8.3, 8.8, 8.9, 8.11
Strength maintenance activity	2.2, 7.10, 8.2, 8.3, 8.4, 8.5, 8.6, 8.7, 8.12, 8.13
Total body workout	8.1, 8.2, 8.3, 8.4, 8.5
Warm-up activities	8.1, 8.2, 8.10, 8.14, 8.16

HOW TO USE THIS BOOK

The *Wrestling Drill Book* includes basic wrestling drills, activities, and contests covering every phase of wrestling. It should be read in its entirety and then kept on hand as a reference source.

Coaches must continually determine whether the drills they use in practice achieve their goals. The drills in this text are useful for evaluating drill design and, because they make practices more stimulating, enhance overall learning and skill development.

Lead-up drills for basic wrestling skills such as takedowns, reversals, escapes, riding, and pinning are found in chapters 1 through 6. Activities beneficial for warm-up and conditioning are in chapter 8, and setup, duckunder, and arm drag drills are in chapter 3. The activities in chapter 7 will particularly interest the peewee and junior high coaches and physical educators because they include many games that can be played on a wrestling mat; many of these activities can also be used to promote interest in wrestling and to make practices more stimulating. Coaches must try to keep practices from becoming boring, because boredom impairs learning and skill development.

Each individual drill or activity is presented and explained using the following format:

Skill Level: The drills have been designed to be used at four different levels of ability: peewee (beginner), junior high (novice to intermediate), senior high (elite), and college. The drills listed for peewee wrestlers could be used by boys in junior or senior high school, but drills should not be used for levels lower than indicated due to the physical and emotional immaturity of the participants.

Purpose: This section of each drill states what the drill is designed to accomplish in terms of wrestling skill acquisition or tactical and technical preparation. For instance, the Power Step Penetration Drill is designed to teach wrestlers a method for attacking an opponent.

Basic Skills: This section lists the basic skills used in performing each drill. In most cases, the USA Wrestling basic skill listings will be named. Those skills are position, motion, level change, penetration, lifting, backstep, and back arch. Other basic skills, including hand control, chaining moves, and hip control, are identified in the chapter introductions. Subskills are listed in parentheses. The Basic Skills listing sometimes reads "N/A" ("not applicable"), especially in chapters 7 (games) and 8 (exercises).

Prerequisite: This section briefly states the skills wrestlers should be able to perform before participating in the drill.

Procedure: This is a step-by-step description of the drill, often illustrated with photographs.

Coaching Points: This section alerts coaches to the key points in each drill. A key point might consist of a slight variation of the drill or include a key concept wrestlers must be made aware of to understand the purpose and structure of a given situation. Sometimes the coaching point simply suggests when to use the drill.

Safety Concerns: Wrestlers should always be grouped according to weight classes to obtain maximum safety during drills and competition. Safety concerns will be noted for any drill that has an increased risk for injury; these explain only the special precautions the coach should take.

CHAPTER 1

LEG ATTACK DRILLS

Single and double leg attacks have always been deemed the most effective takedown maneuvers for high school and college wrestlers. Currently they are also premier maneuvers in international competition. To be successful with these takedowns, the wrestler must maintain proper stance or position, create motion, lower levels, and penetrate through the opponent. This chapter's drills reinforce four of the seven basic skills: position, motion, level change, and penetration.

These drills are lead-up activities for the development of successful single leg, double leg, high-crotch, and other variations on the leg attack including foot sweeps and ankle picks.

Proper stance is important so that the wrestler can defend himself and start an offensive attack of his own. The stance drills are followed by movement drills, for a wrestler who is unable to create motion will find it difficult to score an offensive takedown. The movement drills are designed to teach the wrestler to create an angle on his opponent and effectively attack him. A high percentage of wrestlers who score the first takedown in a match will win, so a wrestler should constantly be moving and on the attack. The successful leg attack must also include changing of levels. The level-change drills stress bending at the knees. Wrestlers must be cautioned against bending at the waist to change levels, as this can result in having one's face snapped into the mat. The chapter concludes with penetration drills and lead-up activities for foot sweeps and ankle picks.

Effective practice of these drills should increase wrestlers' success rates with the leg attack, whether at the peewee, junior high, senior high, or college level.

1.1 STATUE DRILL

Skill Level:
Peewee, junior high, senior high

Basic Skill:
Position

Purpose:
To assume a proper neutral position wrestling stance

Prerequisite:
The wrestlers should have had a proper wrestling stance described and demonstrated for them.

Procedure: The wrestler assumes a proper stance and holds it while you critique him.

Coaching Points: In most stances, the wrestler should have his knees bent, hips square, elbows tight to the body, shoulders and neck rounded forward (like a turtle pulling its head into its shell), and head up. Comment on the stance of each wrestler in the room to assure you've given feedback to all wrestlers and to help everyone feel part of the team.

1.2 TEAM MIRROR DRILL

Skill Level:
Peewee, junior high, senior high, college

Purpose:
To create motion while maintaining a proper stance

Basic Skills:
Position, motion

Prerequisite:
The wrestlers must be able to assume a proper neutral position wrestling stance.

Procedure: The wrestlers assume their stances facing the coach. The captain faces the team and begins side-to-side movement. The team mirrors the captain, changing direction as he does. Throughout the motion drill, each wrestler must maintain a proper stance.

Coaching Points: Demand proper stance throughout this drill.

1.3 SCARECROW DRILL

Skill Level:
Peewee, junior high

Basic Skills:
Position, motion

Purpose:
To create motion in front of a stationary opponent

Prerequisite:
The wrestlers must be able to assume and maintain a proper neutral position wrestling stance.

Procedure: The dark wrestler stands in a scarecrow position with his arms outstretched to the sides. The light wrestler assumes a proper stance and moves from side to side, first directly in front of his opponent, then in front of one arm, and then back to the other arm.

Coaching Points: You might advise the offensive wrestler to feint leg attacks in front of each arm during his side-to-side movement. The feinting can be used as a setup for a leg attack.

1.4 SPREAD EAGLE DRILL

Skill Level:
Peewee, junior high

Basic Skills:
Position, motion

Purpose:
To create motion while maintaining a proper stance

Prerequisite:
The wrestlers should be able to create simple movement while maintaining proper stance.

Procedure: One wrestler lies on the mat in a belly-up, "spread eagle" position. His partner assumes a stance position and begins to move around him, stepping over each leg and each arm as he circles.

SAFETY CONCERNS
Caution the circling wrestlers to be careful not to step on the wrestlers lying on the mat.

1.5 TENNIS BALL MOTION DRILL

Skill Level:

Peewee, junior high

Basic Skills:

Position, motion, level change

Purpose:

To maintain a proper stance while creating motion, with emphasis on keeping the elbows tight to the body

Prerequisite:

The wrestlers must be able to assume a neutral position wrestling stance.

Procedure: The wrestlers are paired and instructed to face each other not more than one arm-length apart. Each wrestler holds a tennis ball in each armpit. One wrestler begins circular motion, changing direction at will. The other wrestler mirrors him, changing direction as he does. Both wrestlers try not to drop the tennis balls.

Coaching Points: Remind wrestlers not to circle so fast that they hop up and down, leaving their legs unprotected.

1.6 MIRROR CIRCLE DRILL

Skill Level:
Peewee, junior high, senior high

Basic Skills:
Position, motion

Purpose:
To react to an opponent's movement

Prerequisite:
The wrestlers should be able to create motion while maintaining a proper stance.

Procedure: The wrestlers are paired and instructed to face each other not more than one arm-length apart. One wrestler begins circular motion, changing direction at will. The other wrestler must attempt to mirror him, changing direction as he does. The roles are reversed in the next session.

Coaching Points: Caution wrestlers not to circle so fast that they begin to hop up and down. Remind them that they must protect their legs in a match situation and therefore should remain in a low, well-protected stance for this drill.

1.7 STANCE MAINTENANCE DRILL

Skill Level:
Peewee, junior high, senior high, college

Basic Skills:
Position, motion, level change

Prerequisite:
The wrestlers must be able to maintain a proper wrestling stance.

Purpose:
To react to an opponent's attack by maintaining a proper stance

Procedure: Wrestlers are paired on their feet, facing each other. One wrestler is assigned to destroy the other wrestler's stance using head bangs, pushes, pulls, forearm shots, and so on. The other wrestler reacts by readjusting his posture to maintain a proper stance. The roles of the wrestlers are reversed in the next session.

Coaching Points: Insist that the offensive wrestler also maintain a proper stance during this drill; remind him that if he uses poor position in practice it may carry over into a match situation.

1.8 SANDBAG STANCE-MAINTENANCE DRILL

Skill Level:
High school, college

Basic Skills:
Position, motion, level change

Purpose:
To maintain a neutral position wrestling stance while being attacked

Prerequisite:
The wrestlers must be able to remain in a low, standing, neutral position wrestling stance.

Procedure: Wrestlers are assigned to face each other on their feet in a proper wrestling stance. The light wrestler uses head bangs and push–pull movements in an attempt to destroy the dark wrestler's base. The dark wrestler carries a sandbag as he attempts to maintain his stance; the additional weight helps strengthen the leg muscles while teaching the wrestler to maintain a proper stance while under attack.

Coaching Points: Remind the wrestlers that they must work much harder to maintain position in this drill because they cannot use their arms to block and balance, but instead must rely heavily on their movement and level change for stance maintenance.

1.9 TENNIS BALL STANCE-MAINTENANCE DRILL

Skill Level:
Peewee, junior high

Basic Skills:
Position, motion, level change

Purpose:
To keep elbows tight to the body while wrestling from the neutral position

Prerequisite:
The wrestler must be able to create motion while maintaining a proper neutral position wrestling stance.

Procedure: Two wrestlers face each other on their feet in proper wrestling stances. The light wrestler holds a tennis ball under each armpit. The dark wrestler is instructed to destroy the light wrestler's stance by using head bangs, push–pulls, and forearm shots. Should the light wrestler drop a tennis ball, it is a signal that he has been forced out of the proper position.

Coaching Points: Demonstrate how an opponent may score by using a duckunder if the wrestler's elbows are not held tight to the body.

1.10 TAP DRILL

Skill Level:
Peewee, junior high, senior high

Basic Skills:
Position, motion, level change

Purpose:
To be able to lower the level for the purpose of attacking an opponent's legs

Prerequisite:
The wrestlers should have been presented with visual and verbal demonstrations of level change methods.

Procedure: The object of this drill is to see how many times a wrestler can tap his opponent's right knee with his right hand in 5 seconds. There are several other similar contests, such as tapping the thigh, calf, ankle, or shoulder. Strategies, such as blocking and penetration, will evolve during this drill.

Coaching Points: Make sure wrestlers understand that they must lower the level by bending at the knees, not at the waist. If a wrestler begins to bend at the waist, allow his opponent to snap him down.

1.11 POWER STEP PENETRATION DRILL

Skill Level:
Peewee, junior high, senior high, college

Basic Skills:
Position, motion, level change, penetration

Purpose:
To effectively attack an opponent's leg

Prerequisite:
The wrestlers should be able to assume a stance, create motion, and change levels.

Procedure: The wrestlers line up in the wrestling room and use the power step for penetration across the length of the mat. A power step is performed by stepping the right toe even with the left heel, lowering the level, and stepping forward with the left foot. In a competitive setting the wrestler would attempt to drive through his opponent or step up and drive across his opponent.

Coaching Points: Be sure the wrestlers maintain proper position with each penetration step—heads up, shoulders over knees, and backs straight.

1.12 SHOESTRING PENETRATION DRILL

Skill Level:
Peewee, junior high, senior high

Purpose:
To be able to effectively attack
an opponent's legs

Basic Skills:
Position, motion, level change,
penetration

Prerequisite:
The wrestlers should be able to
assume a stance, create motion,
and change levels.

Procedure: The dark (defensive) wrestler ties his shoestrings
together and assumes a square stance. The light (offensive) wrestler
lowers his level and penetrates. The lead foot of the light wrestler
must step on or beyond the dark wrestler's shoestring; this assures
the offensive wrestler that he has penetrated deep enough to score
a takedown.

Coaching Points: Insist that the wrestlers step on or beyond the
shoestring, thus assuming the deep penetration needed during competition. Remind wrestlers to be within one bent-arm's length of
the opponent before attacking.

1.13 LEG LIFT PENETRATION DRILL

Skill Level:
Peewee, junior high, senior high, college

Basic Skills:
Position, motion, level change, penetration

Purpose:
To practice penetration skills needed to capture a single leg

Prerequisite:
The wrestlers must be able to assume a stance and penetrate.

Procedure: The light wrestler penetrates toward the left leg of the dark wrestler. The dark wrestler lifts his leg as the light wrestler penetrates; this motion allows the light wrestler to penetrate beyond the leg that is to be captured.

Coaching Points: Remind wrestlers that when they penetrate on an opponent's leg, the leg will usually be moving backward in a sprawl motion, so the penetrating wrestler must penetrate beyond the spot where the leg started.

1.14 SCARECROW DRILL
FOR HIGH-LEVEL PENETRATION

Skill Level:

Peewee, junior high

Purpose:

To create motion and lower the level before penetration

Basic Skills:

Position, motion, level change, penetration

Prerequisite:

The wrestlers should have engaged in stance, motion, and level-change drills.

A

B

Procedure: The dark wrestler assumes a scarecrow position, with both arms outstretched to the sides. The light wrestler executes a high-level penetration step underneath one of the dark wrestler's arms (Figure A). The coach dictates what type of penetration step should be executed.

Coaching Points: Remind the light wrestler that he is penetrating on an imaginary opponent and therefore should visualize the movement in his mind. He should also use the step-up-and-drive movement to finish the drill (Figure B).

1.15 SCARECROW DRILL
FOR LOW-LEVEL PENETRATION

Skill Level:
Peewee, junior high

Purpose:
To create motion and lower the level before penetration

Basic Skills:
Position, motion, level change, penetration

Prerequisite:
The wrestlers must be able to assume a stance, create motion, and change levels.

A

B

Procedure: The defensive wrestler assumes a scarecrow position on his knees, causing the offensive wrestler to execute a low-level penetration step (Figure A).

Coaching Points: Remind the light wrestler that he is penetrating on an imaginary opponent and therefore should visualize the movement in his mind. He should also use the step-up-and-drive movement to finish the drill (Figure B).

1.16 TENNIS BALL
DOUBLE-LEG PENETRATION DRILL

Skill Level:

Peewee, junior high

Purpose:

To keep elbows tight to the body when penetrating on the legs of an opponent

Basic Skills:

Position, motion, level change, penetration

Prerequisite:

The wrestlers must be able to assume a stance, create motion, and lower the level.

Procedure: One wrestler executes double leg penetration shots with tennis balls held underneath his armpits. He must lower the level and penetrate without dropping the tennis balls.

Coaching Points: Have the wrestlers perform the Shoot the Airplane Drill (Drill 4.6) to demonstrate the detrimental effects of penetrating with elbows away from the body.

1.17 T-SHIRT HARNESS DRILL

Skill Level:
Peewee, junior high, senior high

Purpose:
To keep elbows tight to the body when penetrating

Basic Skills:
Position, motion, level change, penetration

Prerequisite:
Wrestlers must be able to assume a stance, create motion, change levels, and penetrate.

Procedure: The wrestler puts a T-shirt over his head and down his back into a position even with his elbows, as shown in the figure. This forces the wrestler's elbows to stay tight to the sides of his body. He faces a partner and begins executing double leg penetration shots.

Coaching Points: Remind the wrestlers that they should lower levels prior to penetration.

1.18 CROSS-ARM REACH PENETRATION DRILL

Skill Level:
Peewee, junior high, senior high, college

Purpose:
To enhance a wrestler's ability to quickly change directions when attacking an opponent and to be set up for the high-crotch takedown

Basic Skills:
Position, motion, level change, penetration, (subskill—change of direction)

Prerequisite:
The wrestlers should be able to assume a stance, create motion, change levels, and penetrate.

A

B

Procedure: The light wrestler assumes a square stance. He lowers his level and uses a cross-arm reach penetration step. The light wrestler penetrates with his right foot, simultaneously attempting to tap dark's upper thigh with his left hand (Figure A). Once the initial penetration has been made, the dark wrestler steps back to avoid having his leg captured. As dark is stepping back, light stands on his right foot and penetrates with his left foot, this time using a right-hand lead (Figure B).

In a match situation the light wrestler would attempt to capture dark's exposed right leg and score a takedown. In this drill, the dark wrestler steps back and the entire routine is performed again. The light wrestler continues this regime for the entire length of the mat. The dark wrestler then becomes the attacker for the return trip across the mat. Ideally a complete takedown should be performed once the wrestlers reach the end of the mat.

Coaching Points: This drill should be done very slowly at first; emphasize body positions. Once positions and techniques improve, emphasize speed of penetration and direction change. Give special notice to light's position upon penetration. His head should be facing up and in, his shoulders should be over his knees, and his reach should not extend past his penetration knee. He must be careful not to overreach, as this could cause him to become overextended and consequently snapped out of position. This drill can also be performed by a single wrestler as a shadow wrestling warm-up drill; remind the wrestler to visualize the actual scoring of a takedown to improve actual motor skill performance.

1.19 SHOESTRING PENETRATION CONTEST

Skill Level:
Peewee, junior high, senior high, college

Purpose:
To simulate a single leg penetration movement in a competitive situation

Basic Skills:
Position, motion, level change, penetration

Prerequisite:
The wrestlers must be able to assume a stance and penetrate.

A

B

Procedure: The object of this contest is for the light wrestler to untie one of the dark wrestler's shoes during a penetration attempt. The light wrestler fakes penetration attempts against his partner's left foot. The dark wrestler blocks at the shoulders and moves his foot backward (Figure A). Once the light wrestler has executed several successful fake attempts, he steps in and unties the dark wrestler's shoe (Figure B).

Coaching Points: Inform the wrestlers that success in this contest will lead to success in penetrating and capturing a single leg. Encourage wrestlers to fake the penetration attempt once, twice, or even three times before actually attempting penetration, to set up the opponent.

1.20 KNEE CHANGE–TURN CORNER DRILL

Skill Level:

Peewee, junior high

Purpose:

To enhance a wrestler's ability to "turn the corner" and create an angle on an opponent when attacking a single leg

Basic Skills:

Position, motion, level change, penetration, (subskill—direction change)

Prerequisite:

The wrestlers must be able to assume a stance, create motion, change levels, and penetrate.

A

B

Procedure:

Shoot-Out (for Primary Wrestlers). The wrestlers line up in two lines facing opposite walls. They are instructed to lower the level and penetrate. They should end up in a position with one knee up and one knee down (Figure A). On command, they have a contest to see how fast they can change knees while they pretend to have a gunfight. The hand that would normally go around the leg is holding the imaginary gun (Figure B).

C

Capture (for Intermediate Wrestlers). The light wrestler attacks a single leg with a high crotch and ends up in a knee up–knee down position. The coach may want to play Shoot-out first or simply have the light wrestler execute a knee change to capture the leg (Figure C).

Capture Fast (for Advanced Wrestlers). The advanced wrestler attacks, executes a knee change, and scores a single leg takedown.

Coaching Points: Advise your wrestlers continually of the importance of direction change for creating an angle when attacking a single leg. Do not let wrestlers become overextended on their penetration attempts or they will not be able to execute a knee change.

1.21 SOLO STEP-AND-DRIVE DRILL

Skill Level:

Peewee, junior high, senior high, college

Purpose:

To teach a wrestler how to stand and drive across an opponent's body to finish a takedown attempt

Basic Skills:

Level change, motion, (sub-skills—direction change and drive across body)

Prerequisite:

The wrestlers should have been presented with visual and verbal demonstrations of a step-and-drive finish.

A

B

Procedure: The wrestler begins in a one-knee-up, one-knee-down position (Figure A). On command, he stands on his left foot and drives across an imaginary opponent (Figure B).

Coaching Points: Emphasize that this drill simulates the action needed to score on a single leg by turning the corner to drive across an opponent's body for a score.

1.22 DRIVE AND LIFT DRILL

Skill Level:
Junior high, senior high, college

Purpose:
To teach a wrestler to combine direction change with a drive and lift combination in order to finish a single or double leg attack

Basic Skills:
Level change, lifting, (sub-skills—direction change and drive across)

Prerequisite:
The wrestlers must be able to penetrate without becoming overextended.

A   B

Procedure: The light wrestler assumes a position on both knees with his right hand up the dark wrestler's crotch and his left arm behind his back (Figure A). Dark holds light's arm behind his back. On command light steps up with his left foot, crosses over into a double leg position with his right arm, and either lifts the dark wrestler or drives him across the mat with his head (Figure B).

Coaching Points: Caution the dark wrestler not to raise the light wrestler's captured arm above 90 degrees of flexion at the elbow joint.

SAFETY CONCERNS
Wrestlers should not wrestle live from this particular position, as injury to the arm might occur.

1.23 INSIDE STEP–TURN CORNER DRILL

Skill Level:
Peewee, junior high, senior high, college

Purpose:
To develop proper penetration and combine that skill with direction change for successful single leg attacks

Basic Skills:
Position, motion, level change, penetration, (subskill—direction change)

Prerequisite:
The wrestlers must be able to penetrate without becoming overextended.

Procedure: Two wrestlers face each other on their feet not more than one arm-length apart. The offensive wrestler executes a right-leg lead penetration step, reaching high into his partner's thigh region. Once penetration has occurred, the defensive wrestler steps in a backward circle motion. Meanwhile, the offensive wrestler brings his left foot up to a position even with his forward foot and changes direction so that he is driving into and across his partner's body. (This motion was used for the step-and-drive maneuver from the previous drill.) He also uses his arms and changes off to a double leg. This sequence of penetrations and corner turns continues for 30 seconds, and then roles are reversed.

Coaching Points: Reinforce the concept that direction change is very important for a successful leg attack.

1.24 THRUST DRILL

Skill Level:
Peewee, junior high, senior high

Purpose:
To counter a defensive wrestler's whizzer attack

Basic Skills:
Penetration, level change, (subskill—direction change)

Prerequisite:
The wrestlers must be able to rotate at the hips, creating a thrust motion with the elbows.

A

B

C

Procedure: There are three phases of this drill. The first phase begins with the light wrestler standing in very poor position on his feet. The dark wrestler leans on him and places his hands (palms) between and blocking against the light wrestler's thighs (Figure A).

On a whistle command, light lowers his level and rotates his hips while using his left elbow to thrust past the dark wrestler's blocking arm. This motion clears light's head to the outside (Figure B). This phase concludes with light using a right-hand high crotch and pivot behind for a score.

The second phase of this drill is to practice the thrust skill when attacking a single leg. The light wrestler locks on a single leg in an overextended position as the dark wrestler counters with a full sprawl and whizzer. (The dark wrestler must not be allowed to attack the head or face.) The light wrestler steps in on his knees and then thrusts out, using a knee change to finish for the score (Figure C).

The final phase of this drill is to work the thrust as soon as the defensive partner begins to sprawl in an attempt to counter the single leg attempt.

Coaching Points: Point out that if a wrestler hits a thrust as soon as his opponent whizzers, he will avoid scramble situations down on the mat.

1.25 FRONT HEADLOCK–SCARECROW DRILL

Skill Level:
Peewee, junior high, senior high

Basic Skills:
Penetration, level change

Purpose:
To teach a wrestler to immediately lunge forward, attempting to capture an opponent's leg, when faced with a front headlock situation

Prerequisite:
The wrestlers must be able to execute a front headlock or at least understand the principles that make it effective.

A

B

Procedure: The dark wrestler assumes a scarecrow position on his knees. The light wrestler begins with his head under one of the dark wrestler's arms (Figure A). This simulates a front headlock position. On a whistle command the light wrestler forces his head back and lunges forward on his knees. This motion brings his base underneath his shoulders (Figure B). Simultaneously he grabs for an imaginary leg, comes to his feet, and drives across his imaginary opponent.

Coaching Points: Remind your wrestlers that they must not become overextended when put in a front headlock situation. This is a good drill for reinforcing that concept.

1.26 DOUBLE-UP DRILL

Skill Level:
Junior high, senior high

Purpose:
To correct the offensive wrestler's overextended body position that has resulted from a defensive sprawl

Basic Skills:
Position, motion, level change, penetration

Prerequisite:
The offensive wrestlers must be able to penetrate using a double leg maneuver, and the defensive wrestlers must be able to execute a sprawl maneuver.

A

B

C

Procedure: The wrestlers assume positions in which the light wrestler is locked on a double leg with his hands behind the knees of the dark wrestler. The dark wrestler is in a one-half sprawl (Figure A). On command, the dark wrestler executes a three-quarter sprawl (Figure B). The light wrestler must pull in with his arms and take a step in and up on his knees. This motion should place his hips in an excellent position for a finish (Figure C). This routine should be performed for 25 to 30 repetitions in a given time period.

Coaching Points: Use this drill for wrestlers who are fatigued. It will simulate that "last shot" often needed to win late in a match.

1.27 FISHHOOK SNAGS DRILL

Skill Level:
Peewee, junior high

Purpose:
To capture a single leg without putting knees on the mat

Basic Skills:
Position, motion, level change, penetration

Prerequisite:
The wrestlers must be able to lower level and penetrate without becoming overextended.

Procedure: The light wrestler fakes a shot on a single leg, then lowers his level and steps his foot toward the dark wrestler. He then pretends that his hands are fishhooks (by cupping his hands and fingers) and snags just behind the knee of the dark wrestler. The fishhook action should snag the two cords located on the back of the knee.

Coaching Points: This is an excellent technique drill for elementary wrestlers, but remind them they must keep their heads up and looking into the chest of their partners so that they do not become overextended. Be sure they bend at the knees, not at the waist, when changing levels.

1.28 LEG PINCH DRILLS

Skill Level:
Peewee, junior high

Purpose:
To control an opponent's leg in a single leg–leg up position without using hands

Basic Skills:
Position, motion, level change, penetration

Prerequisite:
The wrestlers must be able to capture a single leg.

Procedure: The light wrestler captures one of the dark wrestler's legs and pinches it between his own. He must control the captured leg without using his hands. He then creates motion and changes levels, all the time controlling the captured leg with his own leg pinch-off.

Another way to drill this pinch-off is to have races across the mat. One man controls a leg and races across the mat, and then his partner controls his leg for the return trip.

Coaching Points: Have the wrestlers execute a single leg finish at the end of the drill or race. This will simulate and prepare the wrestler for a match situation. Insist that wrestlers maintain a proper stance during this drill.

1.29 SOCCER KICK DRILL

Skill Level:
Junior high, senior high, college

Purpose:
For the offensive wrestlers, to develop proper timing in order to trip an opponent to the mat; for the defensive wrestlers, to maintain balance in a single leg up situation

Basic Skills:
Position, motion, penetration, level change

Prerequisite:
The offensive wrestlers must be able to successfully capture a single leg, and the defensive wrestlers must be able to use a loose whizzer.

Procedure: The light wrestler captures a high single leg and leans back, holding dark's leg high enough to cause dark to hop to maintain balance. Dark is using a loose whizzer for support as he hops. The light wrestler attempts to trip dark by kicking dark's shin while he is in the air. The kick should be executed as if attempting to kick a soccer ball. This drill involves a great amount of timing; if the light wrestler doesn't score on the first kick attempt, he should simply try again.

SAFETY CONCERNS
There is some danger involved in falling to the mat. Therefore, you may wish to have your wrestlers tap the shin area with their feet and not actually bring their partners to the mat each time. Allow wrestlers to move their kneepads to the shins if they wish to, in an attempt to prevent them from becoming bruised.

1.30 FOOT SWEEP DRILL

Skill Level:
Junior high, senior high, college

Purpose:
To develop the rhythm of lifting and blocking in order to score from the neutral position using a foot sweep maneuver

Basic Skills:
Position, motion, level change, penetration

Prerequisite:
The wrestlers must be able to assume a double leg lift position (Figure A).

A

B

Procedure: The light wrestler assumes a double leg lift position. He pivots into the dark wrestler and pulls him in a circle with his right hand. As the dark wrestler hops to maintain his balance, the light wrestler uses a knee block for a takedown (Figure B). This drill helps to teach a wrestler how to set up the sweep by using a circle pull and block.

Coaching Points: Make sure that the wrestlers are merely blocking with their thighs and not using their feet or knees for a tripping motion.

1.31 FOOT SWEEP DANCE

Skill Level:
Junior high, senior high

Purpose:
To develop rhythm for executing
a foot sweep

Basic Skills:
Position, motion, level change,
penetration

Prerequisite:
The wrestlers must be able to
assume an inside biceps control
situation.

Procedure: The light wrestler hop-steps on his left foot while pulling his partner with his right hand, using his right foot to block the
dark wrestler's left shin. He then hop-steps back on his right foot,
pulls with his left hand, and blocks using his left foot. This combination continues for the length of the mat.

Coaching Points: Stress that the wrestler executing the foot sweep
does not need to kick his opponent's shin but only block it with his
foot as he pulls.

1.32 INSIDE-LEG TRIP CONTEST

Skill Level:
Junior high, senior high, college

Purpose:
To practice scoring from the neutral position by using an inside-leg trip maneuver

Basic Skills:
Position, motion, level change, penetration

Prerequisite:
The wrestlers must practice inside-leg trip maneuvers before holding this contest.

Procedure: Two wrestlers face each other with their hands behind their backs. The object is to score using an inside-leg trip, forcing the opponent to the mat. Kicking and spearing with the head are not allowed. If a wrestler bends over to defend himself, he is given one caution and disqualified the next time he does it. If both men fall down, the one who kept his hands locked is declared the winner. This contest could be used to find a champion leg tripper for light-weights, middleweights, and heavyweights.

Coaching Points: It may be wise to use a third wrestler as a referee. He could be in charge of giving cautions for head blocks and would be final judge in case both men fall to the mat.

1.33 ANKLE PICK DRILL

Skill Level:
Peewee, junior high, senior high, college

Basic Skills:
Position, motion, level change, penetration

Purpose:
To create motion by forcing an opponent to move in a circular pattern

Prerequisite:
The wrestlers must be able to control their opponents with a collar tie and wrist control situation.

A

B

Procedure: The light wrestler begins in a collar tie and wrist control situation. He circles to his right, then takes a deep circling step back with his left foot, simultaneously pulling with the wrist control hand. This movement causes the dark wrestler's right foot to step toward the light wrestler (Figure A). The light wrestler then lowers level, pulling dark's head toward his right knee, and uses his left hand to pick behind dark's right heel (Figure B). In a match situation, light would pick the heel and drive the dark wrestler toward his back. In the drill, however, the light wrestler comes back to his feet, circles in the opposite direction, and picks the left heel of the dark wrestler.

Coaching Points: Emphasize how important it is for the wrestler executing the ankle pick to attempt to pull the opponent's head toward his knee, thus creating poor position and allowing the successful pick.

1.34 SPARRING DRILL

Skill Level:

Junior high, senior high, college

Purpose:

For the offensive wrestlers, to use all of the seven basic skills in executing various takedowns and to recognize various situations that might occur during a match situation; for the defensive wrestlers, to present the offensive man with various match-like situations and to execute a two-on-one hand control stand-up immediately following each takedown

Basic Skills:

Position, motion, level change, penetration, back arch, back-stepping, lifting, (subskills—direction change, hand control, and drive across)

Prerequisite:

The wrestlers must be able to execute various takedown maneuvers as well as a stand-up escape.

Procedure: One wrestler executes a setup and a complete takedown. Immediately upon hitting the mat, his partner regains his base and executes a two-on-one hand control stand-up escape. As the wrestlers become more proficient with their takedown maneuvers, the defensive wrestler begins to present various situations for the offensive man to react to.

Coaching Points: This is an excellent way to warm up before actual live competition. It also provides a good cardiovascular workout in any practice setting. As wrestlers improve, insist that they create reaction situations for each other.

CHAPTER 2

UPPER BODY ATTACK DRILLS

The upper body attack is the only attack allowed in Greco-Roman wrestling. The components of the upper body attack are useful for all phases of wrestling. The basic skills of lifting, backstepping, and arching are useful for Greco-Roman and freestyle competition as well as American folkstyle wrestling.

The drills contained in this chapter serve as lead-up activities for the development of a successful upper body attack, which may include such moves as headlocks, bodylocks, saltos, souplesses, and arm throws. As in chapter 1, the actual techniques are not demonstrated; rather, drills are given that can be used as lead-ups for the upper body maneuvers.

The chapter begins with a demonstration of the proper lifting position needed by a wrestler to lift an opponent from the mat, and the various positions from which lifts may be practiced. Then come lead-up activities for the development of the back arch, followed by backstep drills. The chapter concludes with drills that incorporate the lift, backstep, and back arch into an actual throw. In the throwing drills, a throwing dummy or crash pad is used in an attempt to decrease the possibility of injury.

2.1 LIFT DRILLS

Skill Level:

Junior high, senior high, college

Purpose:

To develop proper lifting position to execute basic lifts during competition

Basic Skills:

Position, movement, level change, lifting, back arch

Prerequisite:

The wrestler must have been presented verbal and visual demonstrations of proper lifting techniques. The wrestlers must also possess adequate leg strength to execute the various lifts.

Procedure: Lift drills incorporated into any wrestling practice must emphasize proper lifting position. Figures A and B demonstrate proper lifting positions. In Figure A the wrestler penetrates and lowers his hips. He must then lift his opponent using only his legs and a back arch (Figure B).

There are several positions from which lifts may be performed. The five basic lifts are these:

Side Lift. The light wrestler uses a side bodylock position to lift. The dark wrestler counters with a whizzer (Figures A and B).

A   B

Back Lift. The light wrestler locks around the dark wrestler in a rear standing position. The light wrestler performs the lift by stepping between the dark wrestler's legs, lowering levels, and lifting. This is an essential skill because current rules dictate that a rear standing wrestler must return his opponent to the mat quickly (Figure C).

C

Duck Lift. The light wrestler steps in as if to score on a duckunder. The dark wrestler attempts a neck wrench (Figure D). The light wrestler then slips his collar tie hand to the dark wrestler's biceps while moving his free hand to dark's thigh for a proper lifting position (Figure E).

D

E

High Crotch.   Double leg lift: This lift incorporates the crossover from a high crotch to a double leg. The light wrestler attempts a high crotch. The dark wrestler defends by pushing light's head to the outside (Figure F). Light responds by crossing his right hand across dark's waist, lowering levels, and lifting (Figure G).

F

G

Single Leg Lift.   Lifts may also be executed from a single leg position.

Coaching Points: You might wish to have each lift completed with a bring-to-the-mat finish. Many of the lifts can be finished by using some type of a turk or knee block. However, to save practice time you may want only the last of five lifts completed with some type of bring-to-the-mat.

You may also wish to have lifts executed from a fireman's or a bear-hug position. However, emphasize that in any lift it is mandatory that wrestlers assume proper lifting position: Wrestlers must (a) step into opponent while lowering levels, (b) keep hips lower than the opponent's, and (c) lift using only the legs and a back arch.

2.2 BUDDY SQUAT DRILL

Skill Level:
Junior high, senior high, college

Purpose:
To strengthen the quadriceps muscles

Basic Skills:
Position, level change, penetration

Prerequisite:
The wrestlers must be able to change levels without the added resistance of partners on their backs.

Procedure: The light wrestler assumes a neutral position stance. The dark wrestler then jumps on light's back. The dark wrestler uses a leg pinch as well as a grip around the light wrestler's neck to stay on. The light wrestler should not hold on to the dark wrestler's legs; he keeps his hands forward in a stance position. The light wrestler then does several repetitions of squats as if on a squat rack.

SAFETY CONCERNS
Advise your wrestlers that their knees should not be flexed to or beyond 90 degrees. Recent studies have indicated that squatting beyond 90 degrees may harm the knee joint.

2.3 PUMMELING DRILL

Skill Level:
Junior high, senior high, college

Basic Skills:
Position, movement, level change

Purpose:
To teach wrestlers to keep their elbows tight to their bodies and fight for inside control in an overhook-and-underhook situation

Prerequisite:
The wrestlers must be able to assume an overhook-and-underhook position.

A

B

C

Procedure: Wrestlers face each other in an overhook and under-hook situation (Figure A). To pummel, each wrestler takes his over-hook hand and forces it down between his opponent's underhook and his own body (Figure B), and the wrestlers change head positions from one side to the other (Figure C). The wrestlers then perform the routine to the opposite side. They should begin to keep their arms tight to their sides once they get a feel for the "swimming" action of the pummel.

Coaching Points: This action simulates a match situation. You may wish to end the drill with one wrestler executing a headlock or body-lock. Remind the wrestlers that they must utilize proper wrestling stances and not stand upright.

2.4 PUMMEL CONTEST

Skill Level:

Junior high, senior high, college

Purpose:

To use pummeling maneuvers to get into position to score during competition

Basic Skills:

Position, motion, level change, penetration, lifting, backstep, back arch

Prerequisite:

The wrestlers must be able to execute all of the seven basic skills and have a general knowledge of the basic neutral position scoring maneuvers.

A

B

C

Procedure: The wrestlers begin in an overhook-and-underhook situation. They pummel until actual competition begins on a whistle command. Points are scored as follows: one point for lifting a man off the mat, two points for getting behind an opponent by using a level-change throw-by (Figure A), and one point for snapping the opponent forward so that one hand touches the mat (Figure B). The contest begins with two wrestlers pummeling. They attempt to use a bodylock for a lift or a simple arm throw-by for a go-behind score. The snapdown maneuver is used only when a wrestler is using his head to block (Figure C).

Coaching Points: This drill demands that wrestlers maintain good positions while pummeling. If a wrestler leaves his elbows loose, he will be thrown by; if he blocks with his head, he will be snapped down; and if he doesn't maintain good body position, he will be bodylocked and lifted. This is an excellent Greco-Roman or freestyle game.

2.5 WALL BACKSTEPS DRILL

Skill Level:
Peewee, junior high, senior high, college

Basic Skills:
Position, level change, penetration, backstep

Purpose:
To introduce the actual steps and develop the rhythm needed to complete the initial portion of a backstep maneuver

Prerequisite:
The wrestlers must be able to assume a position and penetrate.

Procedure: The wrestler stands leaning against a wall using his hands for support. His feet are about a foot from the wall. He steps in with his left foot followed by his right foot in a toe–heel position. This step is repeated over and over.

Coaching Points: Have wrestlers practice this drill to the opposite side using a right-foot lead followed by the left foot to a toe–heel position. Stress that the steps are to be completed very slowly at first, speed increasing with time. This is an excellent drill for a wrestler who is resting during round-robin wrestling. You may wish to provide music for this drill.

2.6 RUBBER HOSE BACKSTEP DRILL

Skill Level:
Junior high, senior high, college

Purpose:
To practice the backstep maneuver without a partner

Basic Skills:
Position, level change, penetration, backstep

Prerequisite:
The wrestlers should be able to execute a backstep with a partner.

A

B

C

Procedure: The wrestler first practices the components of a backstep headlock or arm throw using as his partner only an old bicycle innertube or rubber hose tied to a weight machine, a garage door handle, or a set of exercise bars. The wrestler penetrates, completes a backstep (Figure A), forces his hips through on the imaginary opponent (Figure B), and finally pulls the hose in a throwing manner (Figure C). Wrestlers can work on this exercise at home, or it can be made part of a circuit training program in the weight room.

Coaching Points: Remind wrestlers to lower levels for each backstep and to have the hips lower than the imaginary opponent. Encourage wrestlers to visualize the actual scoring maneuver during each repetition.

2.7 HAND-WALK THE WALL DRILL

Skill Level:
Peewee, junior high, senior high, college

Purpose:
To be an introductory activity for the back arch

Basic Skills:
Back arch

Prerequisite:
The wrestlers should be completely warmed up and thoroughly stretched.

Procedure: The wrestler leans backward against a wall, walks down into a back bridge, using only his hands for support, and uses the motor skills needed to perform a back arch.

Coaching Points: Be sure the wrestlers move into a low squat with the hips moving forward as the upper body goes backward.

SAFETY CONCERNS

You may wish to use a spotter for the initial phase of this drill. This would prevent possible neck injury in case the wrestler's hands slip on the wall.

2.8 ROCKING CHAIR DRILL

Skill Level:
Peewee, junior high, senior high, college

Purpose:
To practice the arching motion needed to execute a back arch

Basic Skills:
Motion, back arch

Prerequisite:
The wrestlers should be able to hand-walk down a wall into a back bridge.

A

B

Procedure: This is an individual warm-up drill that begins with the wrestler standing on his knees. He bows his stomach forward, toward the mat, creating a back arch. A side view of the wrestler (Figure A) makes him appear bent like a bow. The hands are placed near the shoulders. The wrestler falls forward in a rocking-chair motion, using his hands to push over into a back bridge (Figure B).

Coaching Points: Have all wrestlers loosen and stretch the lower back region before they attempt this drill.

2.9 HAND GRIP–BACK ARCH DRILL

Skill Level:
Peewee, junior high, senior high, college

Purpose:
To be used as a lead-up activity for executing a back arch

Basic Skills:
Back arch

Prerequisite:
The wrestlers should be able to hand-walk the wall and execute the Rocking Chair Drill.

Procedure: Two wrestlers face each other and grip hands. The light wrestler executes a back arch, while the dark wrestler serves as a safety valve, not allowing the light wrestler to land forcefully on his head. As the light wrestler moves to complete the back arch, he must remember to squat, moving his hips forward as he goes backward. Skill improvement eventually will allow the wrestlers to practice this maneuver using only a single hand grip, and finally to practice the back arch solo.

Coaching Points: Make sure that the partner holding the hands acts as an assistant coach, critiquing each back arch and making suggestions for improvement.

2.10 HIP TOSS DRILL

Skill Level:
Junior high, senior high, college

Purpose:
To be used as a warm-up for backstep maneuvers

Basic Skills:
Penetration, level change, backstep, back arch

Prerequisite:
The wrestlers must be able to execute a backstep.

A

B

C

Procedure: The wrestlers lock up in an overhook-and-underhook situation. The light wrestler uses a right-foot lead backstep (with a right-arm underhook) (Figure A). He then pivots his toes and swivels his hips through and under the dark wrestler's waist (Figure B). This allows him to lift and toss the dark wrestler over onto his feet (Figure C). The dark wrestler then takes his turn and completes a backstep hip toss.

Coaching Points: This is an excellent warm-up drill for backstepping because time isn't wasted getting up off the mat. You might also have your wrestlers use this drill to practice backstep headlocks.

2.11 CRASH PAD DRILLS

Skill Level:
Peewee, junior high, senior high, college

Purpose:
To practice throwing maneuvers without the fear of injury

Basic Skills:
Lifting, backstep, back arch

Prerequisite:
The wrestlers should understand various throwing maneuvers such as headlocks, bodylocks, and arching maneuvers.

A   B

Procedure: The wrestlers stand near a crash pad and perform throwing maneuvers. Wrestlers may practice headlocks, bodylocks, saltos, souplesses, and arm throws by throwing their partners onto crash pads. Figures A and B show examples of throwing onto a crash pad.

Coaching Points: Use this drill for wrestlers who have a fear of throwing or being thrown. Allow wrestlers who wish to use the dummy to do so before actually attempting to throw with a live partner.

2.12 DUMMY DRILLS

Skill Level:
Junior high, senior high, college

Purpose:
To practice the basic skills of lifting, backstepping, and throwing without a partner

Basic Skills:
Position, motion, level change, penetration, lifting, backstep, back arch

Prerequisite:
The wrestlers must have a basic knowledge of each of the techniques to be performed.

Procedure: The following exercises can be performed using a throwing dummy.

Salto. The wrestler locks around the waist of the dummy and performs a back arch (Figure A). This belly-to-belly position is known as a salto and can be used only in freestyle or Greco-Roman competition.

A

Souplesse. The wrestler locks around the waist of the dummy from a rear standing position and performs the back arch (Figure B). This maneuver is also designed only for freestyle or Greco-Roman competition.

B

Arm Throw. The wrestler locks an overhook on the dummy, does a left-foot lead backstep, and finishes with an arm throw (Figure C).

C

Bodylock. The wrestler locks a bodylock on the dummy, penetrates, and then takes the dummy to the mat using a back arch (Figure D).

D

Headlock. The wrestler uses head and arm in combination with a backstep to take the dummy to the mat.

Gut Wrenches. The dummy can also be used to practice "gut wrench" maneuvers used to score tilt points in Greco-Roman and freestyle competition (Figure E).

E

Power Half. The wrestler may practice the power half series on the dummy (Figure F).

F

Lift Drills. The dummy can be used for the drills in Drill 2.1.

Coaching Points: These drills are safe at all levels. The use of a dummy, especially for throwing, allows an inexperienced wrestler to practice the skill without the added fear of injuring a workout partner.

2.13 SLINKY DRILL

Skill Level:
Senior high, college

Basic Skills:
Lifting, back arch

Purpose:
To practice the back arch using a partner for throwing

Prerequisite:
The wrestlers should be able to execute the back arch maneuver using a throwing dummy.

A

B

C

Procedure: The dark wrestler does a handstand facing the light wrestler. The light wrestler locks around the dark wrestler's waist

(Figure A) and begins to execute a back arch. He should execute the back arch very slowly; as he arches back, the feet of the dark wrestler land on the mat before the light wrestler lands on his head in a bridge position (Figure B). The second phase of this drill has the dark wrestler lock around the light wrestler's waist (Figure C), lift him up, and execute the back arch.

SAFETY CONCERNS

If the wrestlers don't keep hold of each other during the drill, there is the possibility of receiving a neck injury. Therefore, this drill should be practiced only by experienced wrestlers.

CHAPTER 3

SETUPS, DUCKS, AND DRAGS

The setup is also important for a wrestler's success when wrestling in the neutral position. Setups are essential for consistency at scoring offensive takedowns. Offensive takedowns are usually preceded by some type of action designed to make the opponent react; head fakes, foot fakes, level changes, motion changes, or push–pull actions are typical tactics for "setting up" the opponent.

In some situations an offensive wrestler will use techniques such as an arm drag or duckunder to set up a possible leg attack. The basic skills involved in executing setups are similar to those used in executing most takedowns—stance, motion, level change, and penetration—and the particular skills needed in each situation vary with the type of setup.

This chapter begins with duckunder and arm drag drills, maneuvers that can be used to set up a single or double leg attack. The chapter then presents setups designed to beat the various arm blocks an opponent might present in a match situation, concluding with a setup circuit in which wrestlers travel around the room using appropriate setups for given situations.

Coaches should continually remind wrestlers that setups are integral to the takedown and require perfect practice. In both practice and match situations, wrestlers should be encouraged to use setups before any takedown attempt.

3.1 KNEE DUCK DRILL

Skill Level:
Peewee, junior high

Purpose:
To teach a wrestler the importance of head rotation when attempting to clear an opponent's arm and body using a duckunder maneuver

Basic Skills:
Position, penetration, (subskill—direction change)

Prerequisite:
The wrestlers should have been presented with verbal and visual demonstrations of a complete duckunder.

A

B

Procedure: The light wrestler begins on his knees with his body bent slightly forward. The dark wrestler drapes his right arm over the head and neck area of the light wrestler (Figure A). On command, the light wrestler steps in on his knees (to get proper hip position), looks toward the ceiling, and then rotates his head toward the dark wrestler (Figure B). This motion should throw the dark wrestler's arm off the light wrestler.

Coaching Points: Use this drill only as a lead-up activity for the younger kids in the program. Remind the wrestlers to "walk in" to improve their hip position before head rotation.

3.2 DUCK STEP DRILL

Skill Level:
Peewee, junior high, senior high, college

Basic Skills:
Position, motion, level change, penetration

Purpose:
To practice level change and the penetration steps needed to execute a duckunder maneuver

Prerequisite:
The wrestlers must be able to assume a stance, lower levels, and penetrate.

Procedure: The light wrestler uses double wrist control from the neutral position and executes penetration for a duckunder. He should duck to one side and then to the opposite side during this routine. The actual drill begins with the light wrestler slapping the dark wrestler's hands together, causing the dark wrestler to react by pulling his arms apart. This reaction should create a little space between dark's arm and side for the light wrestler to duck through. The light wrestler lowers level, penetrates with his left foot to the outside, and then ducks under the dark wrestler's arm. He should look immediately to the ceiling, make a quick position check, and then retreat. The duckunder penetration step is then executed to the opposite side.

Coaching Points: The same drill may be executed with the dark wrestler using hand control or by having light use a collar-to-biceps combination, or with a double inside-biceps combination.

3.3 DUCK PIVOT DRILL

Skill Level:
Peewee, junior high, senior high, college

Purpose:
To teach a wrestler to pivot on his toes

Basic Skills:
Position, motion, level change, penetration, (subskill—direction change)

Prerequisite:
The wrestlers must be able to assume a stance, lower levels, and penetrate.

A

B

C

Procedure: The wrestler assumes a stance resembling a completed duckunder penetration step (Figure A), facing one wall of the wrestling room. The pivot motion is completed by placing the weight on the toes and rotating to the right, facing the opposite wall (Figures B, C). The wrestler then pivots back to his original position.

Coaching Points: This is an excellent drill to incorporate with groin stretching exercises. It not only stretches the groin area but also allows for the pivot motion when changing directions.

3.4 NO-HANDS DUCK–LEVEL CHANGE DRILL

Skill Level:

Peewee, junior high, senior high

Purpose:

To combine and practice motion, level change, penetration, and the head rotation needed to complete a duckunder maneuver

Basic Skills:

Position, motion, level change, penetration

Prerequisite:

The wrestlers must be able to perform a basic duckunder maneuver.

Procedure: The light wrestler assumes a stance with his hands behind his back, while the dark wrestler gets into a normal square stance. The light wrestler then creates movement, lowers level, and executes a penetration step. He uses only his head to duck under dark's arm, and finishes this portion of the drill by rotating his head toward the dark wrestler.

Coaching Points: This is an excellent drill for conditioning a wrestler to maintain his stance, create motion, and score by lowering levels into a head duck. Make sure that wrestlers penetrate by lowering levels at the knees and not by simply bending over at the waist.

3.5 CIRCLE DRAG DRILL

Skill Level:
Peewee, junior high, senior high, college

Basic Skills:
Position, motion, level change, penetration

Purpose:
To counterattack a wrestler who is reaching to block an elbow or shoulder

Prerequisite:
The wrestlers should be able to perform an arm drag maneuver.

Procedure: The dark wrestler reaches with his right arm as if he were going to block light's shoulder. The light wrestler moves his left arm in a motion that simulates rotating an airplane propeller in a counterclockwise motion. Light's motion should block the dark wrestler's wrist area. Light uses his right arm to cup dark's triceps area while lowering levels and penetrating. In a match situation, light might attack a single or double leg or use a leg trip to score. For drill purposes, the dark wrestler steps back and reaches with the opposite arm; this allows the light wrestler to practice the circle drag to the opposite side.

Coaching Points: Insist that your wrestlers use an arm drag any time an opponent reaches in an attempt to block their attacks.

3.6 CHOP DRAG DRILL

Skill Level:
Peewee, junior high, senior high, college

Basic Skills:
Position, motion, level change, penetration

Purpose:
To perform an arm drag when the opponent has blocked low on the elbow or chest area

Prerequisite:
The wrestlers should be able to perform an arm drag maneuver.

A

B

Procedure: The dark wrestler blocks low on the light wrestler's elbow. The light wrestler uses his left hand to chop down (Figure A) on the dark wrestler's wrist. The chop action clears the opponent's arm, allowing for an offensive arm drag attack (Figure B).

Coaching Points: Have your wrestlers practice this setup to both sides of the partner's body.

3.7 BLIND AND DRAG DRILL

Skill Level:
Peewee, junior high, senior high, college

Basic Skills:
Position, motion, level change, penetration

Purpose:
To obtain a reaction from the opponent by momentarily covering his eyes

Prerequisite:
The wrestlers must be able to perform a basic arm drag maneuver.

A

B

C

Procedure: The light wrestler uses his left hand to cover the eye area of the dark wrestler. In most cases the dark wrestler uses his right hand to force the light wrestler's wrist away from his face (Figure A). As the dark wrestler pushes the wrist away, the light wrestler uses the motion to reach into dark's armpit area with his right arm and execute an arm drag (Figure B) while lowering levels, penetrating, and finishing with a right-leg trip (Figure C).

Coaching Points: Be sure the wrestler lowers level and steps in for the trip as soon as the defensive wrestler begins to clear the hand in front of his eyes.

3.8 MOVEMENT AND FOOT FAKE DRILL

Skill Level:

Peewee, junior high, senior high

Purpose:

To use movement along with fake penetration attempts to set up an opponent for a possible takedown

Basic Skills:

Position, motion, level change, penetration

Prerequisite:

The wrestlers must be able to assume a stance and create motion.

Procedure: A wrestler moves in his stance while using his lead foot to fake a shot toward his opponent. The object of the foot fake is to cause his opponent to straighten his legs or momentarily lock his knees, allowing for a successful leg attack.

Coaching Points: Make sure that your wrestlers are always within one bent-arm's length of their opponents before any foot fake or leg attack. This will help prevent overextension during the actual leg attack.

3.9 TAKE CONTROL DRILL

Skill Level:
Peewee, junior high, senior high, college

Basic Skills:
Position, motion, level change, penetration

Purpose:
To set up a wrestler who will not reach, block, or attack and who maintains a good square stance at all times

Prerequisite:
The wrestlers must be able to create movement from a proper stance.

Procedure: This drill is similar to the Stance Maintenance Drill (Drill 1.7). In this situation one wrestler is instructed to maintain a perfect square stance while his partner attempts to move him out of position. The object is to snap, push–pull, and create motion in an attempt to make the opponent reach or step out of position. The offensive wrestler may then lower levels, penetrate, and hopefully score a takedown.

Coaching Points: Insist that the wrestler not forfeit good position while attempting to force his opponent out of position. Acquiring a habit of poor position in practice might allow an opponent to score in a match situation.

3.10 CLEAR THE ARMS DRILL

Skill Level:
Junior high, senior high, college

Purpose:
To enable a wrestler to identify what type of arm block or tie-up is being used by an opponent and how to effectively score in the various situations

Basic Skills:
Position, motion, level change, penetration

Prerequisite:
The wrestlers must be able to create movement from a proper stance.

Procedure: The coach commands one of five movements from the dark defensive wrestler: high shoulder block, low shoulder block, block outside arm, block inside arm, or elbow post. Dark acts, and the light offensive wrestler then uses the proper reaction to clear the block and attack. The following is a list of responses to the given situations.

Beating a High Shoulder Block. The dark wrestler uses a high shoulder block (Figure A). The light wrestler forms a *V* with his left hand, lowers his level, and bumps the dark wrestler's arm off his shoulder (bumping at or above his opponent's elbow). Once the light wrestler has cleared the arm, he is able to attack the dark wrestler's legs.

A

Beating a Low Shoulder Block. The dark wrestler uses a low shoulder block (Figure B). The light wrestler uses a left-hand chop-down. Light's outside-in–chop-down motion clears the dark wrestler's arm and enables light to lower levels and penetrate (Figure C).

B   C

Beating Fingers Outside Arm. When the dark wrestler blocks at the biceps area with his fingers to the outside, the light wrestler reacts with an elbow lift for a high crotch (Figure D).

D

Beating Inside Arm Block. The dark wrestler blocks inside the light wrestler's arm. This action causes the light wrestler to react with a Russian two-on-one (Figure E).

E

Beating an Elbow Post. The dark wrestler uses an elbow post to block the light wrestler. The light wrestler counters with a combination chop and arm drag (Figure F). This maneuver allows the light wrestler to lower levels and penetrate on the legs of the dark wrestler.

F

Coaching Points: You may find that your wrestlers are totally confused when they first practice these skills. If so, practice each block until the responses are mastered. Don't give up; their ability to read and react to situations will improve with practice.

3.11 REACTION CIRCUIT DRILL

Skill Level:
Junior high, senior high, college

Purpose:
To teach a wrestler to recognize various situations he may encounter during a match and how to score against them

Basic Skills:
Position, motion, level change, penetration, lifting, backstep

Prerequisite:
The wrestlers should be able to recognize the various situations they will face in this circuit.

Procedure: The coach posts a sign at each station of the circuit indicating the reaction situation for that station. The sign explains the defensive wrestler's action as well as a way to score against that action. The defensive wrestlers stay at particular stations while the offensive wrestlers travel around the circuit. The offensive wrestlers remain at each station for 15 seconds, rotating to the next station on the coach's whistle. After a complete cycle, the offensive and defensive wrestlers switch roles and the new offensive wrestlers travel the circuit. The following is a typical reaction setup circuit:

Station	Defensive Wrestler's Action	Offensive Wrestler's Reaction
1	Double shoulder block	V the hands and double
2	High shoulder block (1 hand)	V to high crotch or single
3	Low shoulder block (1 hand)	Chop drag to single
4	Reaches toward shoulder	Circle drag to single, double, or trip
5	Grabs both wrists	Clap together to duck-under
6	Head tie	Two on one or reverse duck
7	On one or both knees	Snap, shuck, or shrug
8	Force in with underhook	Fireman's or pummel

Coaching Points: This circuit teaches wrestlers how to react to given situations. Encourage the wrestlers to become familiar with the action–reaction signs before actual practice, using mental imagery as they study the signs.

3.12 AGGRESSIVE SETUP CIRCUIT

Skill Level:

Junior high, senior high, college

Purpose:

To practice various setups for takedowns that are designed to be used against a wrestler who maintains a good square stance

Basic Skills:

Position, motion, level change, penetration, lifting, backstep, back arch

Prerequisite:

The wrestlers must be able to perform basic setup and takedown maneuvers.

Procedure: The coach posts signs at stations in the wrestling room indicating various setups and particular takedowns to be used with those setups. The wrestlers are divided into two groups, with one group remaining at the stations and assuming square stances. The other group travels the circuit in 15-second intervals, performing the prescribed setups and takedowns. The coach's whistle signals rotation to the next station. Once the first group has completed all of the stations, the groups switch roles. A setup circuit might include the following activities:

Station	Offensive Setup	Projected Finish
1	Foot fake	Single, double
2	Level change	Single, double, duck, fire
3	Blind and drag	Drag to trip, single, or double
4	Collar tie–wrist control	Duckunder, single, double
5	Collar tie and motion	Ankle picks
6	Push–pull	Fireman's, single, double, duck
7	Baseball tie	Single, high crotch
8	Underhook	High crotch, ankle pick, headlock, hip toss, bodylock

Coaching Points: Insist that the wrestlers who remain at the stations act as assistant coaches, giving constructive criticism upon completion of each setup and completed takedown. This type of a circuit forces each wrestler to practice all of the setups you've chosen. The individual wrestler will develop one or two favorites, which he will hopefully develop to perfection.

3.13 ADAM DRILL

Skill Level:

Peewee, junior high, senior high, college

Purpose:

To practice takedown setups and takedown maneuvers without an actual partner

Basic Skills:

Stance, position, motion, level change, penetration, lifting, back-step, back arch

Prerequisite:

The wrestlers should be able to perform basic wrestling maneuvers from the neutral position.

Procedure: A wrestler simply performs takedown setups and takedowns on the Adam takedown machine, which is permanently attached to a wall.

Coaching Points: This machine is an excellent device for injured wrestlers to use during practice.

Author's Note: For more information on the Adam Takedown Machine (which was invented by Carl Adams) contact Wayne Endres, 4495 N.W. 1st St., Des Moines, Iowa 50313

CHAPTER 4

NEUTRAL POSITION DEFENSIVE DRILLS

The ability to defend against attack is the final ingredient for success when competing in the neutral position. This chapter's drills center around the three basic lines of defense. The first line of defense is to stop or at least slow an opponent's penetration; these drills involve various elbow blocks, snaps, and a basic hip thrust. The second line of defense is to free one's legs once the opponent has executed a successful penetration attempt; these drills use sprawl maneuvers to destroy the opponent's base by causing him to become overextended.

The final line of defense is to begin a counterattack. Drills designed to score on the opponent once his penetration has been slowed and his base has been destroyed include front headlock and butt drag situations. The three lines of defense could be considered subskills of basic skills needed to compete in the defensive portion of neutral-position wrestling, so the subskills of slowing penetration, freeing the leg, and counterattacking are added to the Basic Skills sections of this chapter.

This chapter also includes drills for snapdowns, sprawling, front headlocks, butt drags, and whizzers. A wrestler who practices these drills perfectly should be able to successfully defend himself when competing in the neutral position.

4.1 HIP THRUST DRILL

Skill Level:
Junior high, senior high

Purpose:
To teach a wrestler how to use a basic hip thrust to stop or slow an opponent's penetration

Basic Skills:
Position, motion, level change, (subskill—slow penetration)

Prerequisite:
The wrestlers must be able to perform double leg penetration.

Procedure: The dark wrestler attempts a half-speed double leg penetration shot. The light wrestler lowers his level and uses his hips to force into the dark wrestler's shoulder area. The thrust action consists of the hips going forward, creating an arch in the back. The dark wrestler then attacks one leg so that the light wrestler can practice using a single hip thrust.

Coaching Points: Have your wrestlers execute this drill for several repetitions before the Sprawl Drill (Drill 4.2). It can also be incorporated into the Sprawl Drill.

4.2 SPRAWL DRILL

Skill Level:
Peewee, junior high, senior high, college

Purpose:
To teach a wrestler how to free his leg after it has been captured by an opponent

Basic Skills:
Position, level change, (sub-skills—slow penetration, freeing the leg)

Prerequisite:
The wrestlers must be able to perform single and double leg penetration shots.

Procedure: There are several ways to drill the sprawl. This drill has the following three phases.

Shadow Sprawl. The wrestlers move from side to side in their stances. The coach feints a shot toward the group. The wrestlers immediately sprawl back, dropping to the mat. (The wrestlers should be advised to drop one hip more than the other, to simulate defending against a single leg shot.)

No-Hands Sprawl. This phase involves using a partner, who makes an actual leg attack. The dark wrestler shoots a single, and the light wrestler sprawls using only his hips (no hands) to counter (Figure A). The hip of the leg being attacked is dropped much lower than the other hip.

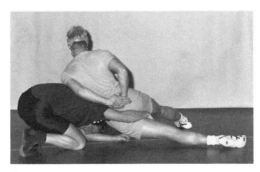

A

Full Contact Sprawl. The dark wrestler attacks a single or double leg. The light wrestler sprawls his hips back and down while counterattacking with a whizzer and a head push-away (Figure B).

B

Coaching Points: You may want to start by exposing your wrestlers to the Hip Thrust Drill (Drill 4.1) before beginning the Sprawl Drill. The Give Ground Drill (Drill 4.3) is a very beneficial exercise for the wrestler to learn next.

4.3 GIVE GROUND DRILL

Skill Level:
Junior high, senior high, college

Purpose:
To teach a wrestler to give ground instead of giving up a takedown when defending himself in the neutral position

Basic Skills:
Motion, level change, (subskill—freeing the leg)

Prerequisite:
The wrestlers should be able to execute single and double leg takedown maneuvers and have a general knowledge of the sprawl defense.

A

B

Procedure: Wrestlers are paired facing each other on their feet. One wrestler (dark) attacks a double leg and continues to drive through his partner. The light wrestler sprawls (Figure A) until dark walks him into a near-standing position. At this point, light must give ground or be taken down. Giving ground simply means that he must throw his legs in a backward motion (Figure B). This movement pattern continues across the length of the mat; dark walks in and up on a double leg attack, light gives ground, and so on. Once the wrestlers near the opposite wall, the coach instructs the light wrestler to score using a butt drag or front headlock counterattack.

Coaching Points: Make sure your wrestlers realize the importance of giving ground. Before completing this drill, you may want the man using the double leg to score, thus demonstrating why ground must be given.

4.4 TENNIS BALL SPRAWL DRILL

Skill Level:
Peewee, junior high

Purpose:
To improve movement time in the sprawl

Basic Skills:
Position, motion, level change, (subskill—freeing the leg)

Prerequisite:
The wrestlers must be able to assume a neutral position wrestling stance.

Procedure: This drill begins with each wrestler holding a tennis ball under each armpit and assuming a neutral position wrestling stance. On a whistle command, the wrestlers drop the balls and attempt to sprawl in a back-and-downward motion to the mat before the balls hit the mat.

Coaching Points: This drill is excellent for breaking the monotony of the daily routine. However, this drill is time consuming and the wrestlers will eventually become bored, so it should only be used once or twice per season.

4.5 SNAPDOWN DRILL

Skill Level:
Peewee, junior high, senior high, college

Purpose:
To learn to change levels and destroy an opponent's penetration attempt with an elbow block and then score using a snapdown maneuver

Basic Skills:
Position, motion, level change, (subskills—slow penetration, counterattack)

Prerequisite:
The wrestlers should have been presented with verbal and visual presentations of the entire snapdown maneuver.

A

B

C

Procedure: The dark wrestler is upright on his knees, leaning slightly forward. The light wrestler will perform the snapdowns. He delivers a blow with his left forearm to dark's right collarbone area; his right hand (thumb down) blocks dark in the shoulder–armpit area (Figure A). This motion helps to destroy or slow an opponent's penetration. Once the block has been delivered, light lets both hands slide past dark's head and shoulder (Figure B). The snapdown portion of this drill is completed by having light cup his hands behind dark's head and armpit, snapping in a downward, to-the-side motion (Figure C). This motion should allow the light wrestler to spin to the opposite side for a score.

Coaching Points: This drill could also be expanded to include snaps and shrugs to either side. Snap-shrugs are accomplished by directing the head in the direction opposite to the spin. This drill can also be incorporated with the Snapdown Spin Drill (Drill 5.5).

4.6 SHOOT THE AIRPLANE DRILL

Skill Level:

Peewee, junior high, senior high

Purpose:

To counter the double leg attack of an opponent who penetrates with his elbows away from his body

Basic Skills:

Position, motion, level change, (subskill—counterattack)

Prerequisite:

The wrestlers must be able to execute double leg penetration.

A

B

Procedure: The offensive (dark) wrestler attempts a double leg penetration shot with his arms out to the side much like airplane wings. As the offensive wrestler penetrates, the defensive (light) wrestler lowers his level and stops the momentum with an overhook–underhook combination (Figure A). The light wrestler pancakes the dark wrestler to his back (Figure B).

Coaching Points: Peewee wrestlers may want to make airplane noises upon penetration, complete with crash and burn sounds as they go to their backs. In fact, many varsity wrestlers will enjoy making the same sounds.

4.7 THREE-MAN FRONT HEADLOCK DRILL

Skill Level:

Senior high, college

Purpose:

To develop proper downward pressure needed to overextend an opponent and to successfully perform a front headlock

Basic Skills:

Position, motion, level change, (subskill—counterattack)

Prerequisite:

The wrestlers should have been presented with verbal and visual demonstrations of the front headlock.

Procedure: The figure shows the three-wrestler alignment needed to perform this drill. The third wrestler maintains a rear standing position with his hands locked around dark's waist. The light wrestler puts a front headlock on the dark wrestler. The objective is for the light wrestler to pull the dark wrestler's face to the mat. Meanwhile, the rear standing wrestler attempts to hold the dark wrestler off of the mat. This is not a pleasant drill for the man in the middle, but it is effective for learning the downward pressure needed for executing a front headlock.

Coaching Points: Because this is unpleasant for the participant in the middle, let only rugged, experienced wrestlers play that role.

4.8 FRONT HEADLOCK–THROW-BY DRILL

Skill Level:
Junior high, senior high, college

Basic Skills:
Motion, (subskill—counterattack)

Purpose:
To overextend an opponent, create motion after capturing a front headlock, and react to the opponent's movements

Prerequisite:
The wrestlers must be able to apply the front headlock maneuver.

A

B

C

Procedure: The light wrestler captures a front headlock off a failed shot from the dark wrestler, then immediately overextends the dark wrestler and begins circling to the left. How he scores depends on the dark wrestler's reaction. If dark attempts to force to the inside the elbow that is over his head, then light throws him by to the left (Figure A). If dark attempts to force that elbow to the outside, light stops and throws dark's head and arm in the opposite direction (to the right) (Figure B).

Coaching Points: Be sure the wrestlers overextend their partners before they begin to circle and create motion. In a match situation, an opponent may be able to walk in on his knees and capture a leg if he is not overextended. You may wish to add a thigh block to this drill once the throw-bys are mastered (Figure C).

4.9 BUTT DRAG–HIGH LEG DRILL

Skill Level:
Junior high, senior high, college

Purpose:
To use direction change in defending against a single leg

Basic Skills:
Position, motion, (subskills—freeing the leg, counterattack)

Prerequisite:
The wrestlers must be able to perform a high-leg over and butt drag maneuvers.

A

B

C

Procedure: The dark wrestler locks onto one leg of the light wrestler. Dark is overextended to simulate a poor shot and an effective sprawl by the light wrestler. In the first phase of this drill, light uses his right hand to reach over the top of dark's neck and grab his right armpit. Light's left hand reaches into the crotch area. Light attempts to pull himself around behind dark using the right-hand arm drag and the left-hand crotch pull (Figure A) and uses a right-leg high-leg over to try to break the dark wrestler's grip (Figure B). In the second phase of this drill the light wrestler uses a left-leg high-leg over to break the dark wrestler's grip on his leg (Figure C). He then spins to the opposite side for a score. The left-leg high leg would be used only after the right-leg high leg has failed. This drill is conducted continuously for 30 seconds, using a butt drag to one side and a high leg to the opposite side.

Coaching Points: Make sure each wrestler reaches over the top of his partner's head and not under his neck. If a wrestler reaches under the neck in an attempt to butt drag his opponent, he will be setting himself up for a sucker drag.

4.10 BUTT DRAG THE TABLE DRILL

Skill Level:
Peewee, junior high, senior high

Basic Skills:
Motion, (subskill—counterattack)

Purpose:
To use a butt drag for a defensive score

Prerequisite:
The wrestlers must be able to perform a butt drag maneuver.

Procedure: One wrestler attempts to maintain a tabletop position (down referee's position) and may circle only to avoid being scored upon. The top man executes as many butt drags as possible in a given time period. The roles are then reversed. The winner is the one who scores the most times.

Coaching Points: Remind the bottom man that he may not use his hands to prevent being scored upon.

4.11 WHIZZER DRILL

Skill Level:
Peewee, junior high, senior high, college

Purpose:
To give the defensive wrestler another weapon to prevent his opponent from attacking and successfully scoring on a leg attack

Basic Skills:
Position, motion, level change, (subskill—freeing the leg)

Prerequisite:
The wrestlers should have been presented with visual and verbal demonstrations of the whizzer maneuvers.

A

B

C

D

Procedure: The light wrestler assumes a position on all fours. The dark wrestler hooks light's left leg and places his right arm across his back. The light wrestler then makes a windmill action with his left arm, attaining a whizzer position (Figure A). This alignment now becomes a scrimmage situation. Light attempts to hip into dark

(Figure B) while straightening his captured leg. He must then sit the captured leg to the front (Figure C) and face his opponent. The dark wrestler meanwhile attempts to keep the leg hooked. Coaches may wish to allow the light wrestler to execute a pancake (Figure D) as he squares to the front.

Coaching Points: You may wish to allow the dark wrestler to use whizzer counters such as a limp arm or an alligator roll-through to score the actual takedown.

4.12 DEFENSIVE CIRCUIT DRILL

Skill Level:

Junior high, senior high, college

Purpose:

To recognize various attacks that may be used in a match situation and how to properly defend against them

Basic Skills:

Position, motion, level change, penetration, lifting, backstep, back arch, (subskills—slow penetration, freeing the leg, counterattack)

Prerequisite:

The wrestlers must be able to recognize the attacks to be used in the circuit and how to effectively defend against them.

Procedure: This circuit is similar to the setup circuits in that half the wrestlers stay at particular stations while the rest travel from station to station. After a complete circuit, the two groups exchange roles.

Station	Offensive Action (Stationary group)	Defensive Reaction (Traveling group)
1	Single leg shot	Sprawl, butt drag
2	Double leg shot	Snapdown and spin
3	On mat, leg hooked, arm across back	Whizzer counter and pancake
4	Single leg up captured	Pull up to clear *or* force head outside and and kickover cradle
5	Headlock	Step to front and throw
6	Bodylock attempt	Metzgar
7	Ankle pick	Shuck by
8	Whizzer	Whizzer counter (limp arm, etc.)

Coaching Points: The stationary man should act as an assistant coach, giving constructive criticism on each wrestler's reaction at his station. You may alter the circuit drill to meet your team's needs.

4.13 ATTACK–COUNTERATTACK DRILL

Skill Level:
Peewee, junior high, senior high, college

Purpose:
To begin a counterattack immediately after an opponent's penetration has been stopped

Basic Skills:
Position, motion, level change, slow penetration, (subskills—freeing the leg, counterattack)

Prerequisite:
The wrestlers should have a basic knowledge of both offensive and defensive scoring maneuvers.

Procedure: The dark wrestler attempts a double leg attack. The light wrestler stops the penetration with an elbow block–snap combination. As dark begins to return to his neutral stance, light is instructed to attack using his own double or single leg shot.

Coaching Points: A wrestler has many opportunities in a match situation in which he may be able to score immediately following his opponent's failed attack. This drill helps accustom wrestlers to this fact.

CHAPTER 5

TOP MAN DRILLS

In collegiate, freestyle, and Greco-Roman wrestling, total time spent wrestling from the advantage position is steadily on the decline. Freestyle and Greco-Roman rules clearly limit the time that may be spent in the advantage position without scoring points. In folk-style wrestling, college and high school wrestlers are often more than willing to play the two-for-one takedown game, working for bonus decisions rather than for the actual fall. However, pinning is still the name of the game! It is indeed the talented, dominant grappler who can ride an opponent and eventually force him into the submission of a fall.

The basic skills needed for advantage wrestling are not clearly defined but might center around the ability of the top man to destroy the bottom man's base by continually controlling his hip movement and his hip position.

This chapter includes riding drills, such as spinning and floating (reaction) drills, and pinning drills, such as cradle and leg drills. There are also several contests that stress the tilting of an opponent.

This chapter's drills will help improve the top man's ability to ride, turn for back points, and finally (hopefully) pin an opponent.

5.1 BASIC SPIN DRILL

Skill Level:
Peewee, junior high, senior high, college

Purpose:
To enhance the top man's ability to move around an opponent

Basic Skills:
Motion

Prerequisite:
None

Procedure: This drill promotes swift mobility for the offensive wrestler while creating an awareness of points of attack from the top position. The drill begins with wrestlers in an up–down referee's position. On a whistle command, the light wrestler begins to spin around the dark wrestler. Light's chest is positioned on the small of dark's back. While the light wrestler spins, he attacks various body parts of the defensive wrestler. For instance, when he circles around dark's head, he may push the head down or attack under an armpit. He can also attack under an arm and pick an ankle when at the side, or use a double underhook from the back.

Coaching Points: Make your wrestlers aware of which body parts might be attacked during the spinning motion.

5.2 BACK-TO-BACK SPIN DRILL

Skill Level:
Peewee, junior high, senior high, college

Purpose:
To enhance a wrestler's balance while using a high-leg over maneuver during the spin drill

Basic Skills:
Position, motion

Prerequisite:
Wrestlers must be able to perform a high-leg maneuver.

Procedure: This drill is performed in the same manner as the Basic Spin Drill (5.1), except that light does not attack dark's body parts. Instead, light begins to spin around in a chest-on-back position. He executes a high-leg over maneuver (Drill 6.16), which brings him into a back-to-back position. Light continues to spin and does another high-leg over into a chest-on-back position. The light wrestler may not use his hands for this drill, as it is a balance drill.

Coaching Points: Make sure your wrestlers practice the high-leg over maneuvers before attempting this drill.

5.3 REACTION SPIN DRILL

Skill Level:
Peewee, junior high, senior high, college

Purpose:
To allow the top man to react to a given situation while spinning

Basic Skills:
Motion

Prerequisite:
Wrestlers should be able to spin around an opponent.

Procedure: The Basic Spin Drill (Drill 5.1) is expanded here to include reaction. The coach may choose to blow a whistle indicating that the light wrestler should reverse the direction of his spin. A more realistic reaction drill is illustrated in the figure. The dark (down) wrestler raises an arm to prevent the light wrestler from spinning around. Immediately, the light wrestler must react by changing directions and spinning in the opposite direction for a simulated score.

Coaching Points: You might want to use a whistle command for direction change at the beginning of the drill. For a more realistic situation, encourage the down man to lift an arm to stop the spin-around, forcing the top man to spin in the opposite direction.

5.4 LIVE SPIN DRILL

Skill Level:
Peewee, junior high, senior high, college

Purpose:
To engage in scramble wrestling situations

Basic Skills:
Position, motion, (subskills— hand control, hip control, and chaining)

Prerequisite:
The wrestlers should be able to perform the Basic Spin Drill (Drill 5.1) and have a basic knowledge of top and bottom man maneuvers.

Procedure: The entire series of spin drills may be expanded to include live wrestling. Near the end of a spin drill, the coach blows a whistle indicating that the wrestlers should wrestle live. This provides scramble-situation wrestling.

Coaching Points: You might want to use this drill as a contest to see whether the bottom man can score an escape or a reversal.

5.5 SNAPDOWN SPIN DRILL

Skill Level:
Peewee, junior high, senior high, collge

Purpose:
To combine the Basic Spin Drill (Drill 5.1) with the Snapdown Drill (Drill 4.5)

Basic Skills:
Position, motion, level change

Prerequisite:
The wrestlers must be able to perform the Basic Spin Drill.

Procedure: The wrestlers face each other with one wrestler on his knees and the other in a neutral position wrestling stance. Upon command the standing wrestler executes a snapdown–spin-around maneuver.

Coaching Points: Constantly remind your wrestlers to look for a spin-around immediately following any snapdown maneuver.

5.6 FLOATING DRILL

Skill Level:
Peewee, junior high, senior high, college

Purpose:
To allow the top man to react to the bottom man's movements

Basic Skills:
Position, motion

Prerequisite:
The wrestlers should be able to perform basic top and bottom man maneuvers.

Procedure: The light wrestler begins on top in a chest-on-back position with his hands under the dark wrestler's armpits. The bottom man completes a series of moves as the top man reacts. The moves and countermoves involved in a short series might include switch–reswitch, roll–reroll, sit-out–spin behind, sit-out–drag around, stand-up–back-heel trip, and Granby–log roll.

Coaching Points: Make up any routine you wish. But be sure to encourage the wrestlers to move at full speed, both when acting and when reacting. This will insure full speed transfer into a match situation.

5.7 FROG IN–BUMP DOWN DRILL

Skill Level:

Peewee, junior high

Purpose:

To increase the top man's ability to destory the bottom man's base immediately following a whistle start

Basic Skills:

Position, motion, (subskill—hip control)

Prerequisite:

The wrestlers must be able to assume an up–down referee's position.

Procedure: The wrestlers assume an up–down referee's position. The top man is told to pretend he is a frog. He uses his legs to drive into the bottom man much as a frog would to leap. The top man may use his arms to block under an arm on the near side and under the thigh on the far side. On a whistle command, the top man leaps into the bottom man and knocks him off of his base.

Coaching Points: Be sure your wrestlers understand that it is very important to destroy the bottom man's base as soon as the whistle blows. It might be advisable to make this a 10-second whistle drill.

5.8 RIDE THE BARREL CONTEST

Skill Level:
Junior high, senior high

Basic Skills:
Position, motion

Purpose:
To allow the top man to maintain control without destroying the bottom wrestler's base

Prerequisite:
The wrestlers must be able to perform rolls and elevators.

A

B

Procedure: The wrestlers begin with the dark wrestler in the down referee's position and the light wrestler on top with his arms around dark's waist but not locked (Figure A). The object of this contest is for the bottom man to attempt to pull the top man into a position where his hip, buttocks, or shoulders touch the mat. Each time one of these body parts touches the mat, a point is scored. The bottom man may use rolls or elevators to score, while the top man counters using only rotation and a leg post (Figure B). The top man may deduct a point from the bottom man's score if he can successfully reroll and remain in a parallel position. However, in this situation, should the bottom man get perpendicular during the reroll, he (the bottom man) scores a point (see Drill 6.18). The roles are reversed for the next timed session.

Coaching Points: Give some type of reward for the winner, or the wrestlers may not keep true scores.

5.9 RIDE AT ALL COSTS CONTEST

Skill Level:
Junior high, senior high

Basic Skills:
Position, motion

Purpose:
To practice maintaining control of an opponent by utilizing counter-maneuvers rather than breaking him flat on the mat

Prerequisite:
The wrestlers must be able to execute basic bottom man maneuvers and their counters.

Procedure: The bottom man is assigned to use any moves except for a stand-up to score an escape or reversal. The top man is told to ride the bottom man using only counters to his moves; he is not allowed to score breakdowns. The combinations might include the switch–reswitch, roll–reroll, sit–spin-around, and Granby–log roll.

Coaching Points: This is a live wrestling situation, and again you should give some type of reward to assure maximum effort.

5.10 CALF ROPING DRILL

Skill Level:
Junior high, senior high

Purpose:
To utilize skills needed for tilting an opponent from the two-on-one near-arm chop position

Basic Skills:
Position, motion, (subskill—hip control)

Prerequisite:
The wrestlers must be able to perform a two-on-one near-arm tilt.

A

B

Procedure: One wrestler is the calf and attempts to run on his hands and knees the length of the wrestling room without being tilted. The other wrestler is the cowboy; he starts in a hover position over the calf (Figure A). As the contest begins, the cowboy attempts to do a near-arm chop with a two-on-one tilt. The cowboy is not allowed to tackle the calf—he must hover and use the near-arm chop (Figure B).

SAFETY TIPS
This drill is relatively safe, but do not allow the top man to use a tackle for a breakdown.

5.11 STEER WRESTLING CONTEST

Skill Level:
Peewee, junior high, senior high

Basic Skills:
Position, motion

Purpose:
To utilize skills needed to perform a spiral ride

Prerequisite:
The wrestlers must be able to perform a spiral ride.

A

B

Procedure: One wrestler starts on his hands and knees as the bull. The other wrestler starts in a hover position with one underhook in place (Figure A). The object is for the bull to run the length of the room on his hands and knees without being turned toward one of the side walls. The top man uses his underhook (Figure B) arm to run a spiral and force the bottom man to face a side wall. The top man must run toward the bottom man's head to turn him toward a wall, just as he would have to do to break down an opponent for a spiral ride.

Coaching Points: This contest will provide a welcome relief from the normal daily routine of practice. Remind the top man to always run toward the head when attempting to score a breakdown using a spiral.

5.12 CRADLE FLOATING DRILL

Skill Level:
Peewee, junior high, senior high

Basic Skills:
Position, motion

Purpose:
To create an awareness of the opportunities available for the top man to apply a near- or far-side cradle

Prerequisite:
The wrestlers must be able to perform near- and far-side cradle maneuvers.

Procedure: This drill is similar to the Floating Drill (Drill 5.6), except the top man is continually attempting to lock up a cradle. The dark wrestler does a series of sit-outs and/or starts numerous stand-ups. The light wrestler rides from the back in a chest-on-back position with hands underneath the dark wrestler's armpits. Each time the bottom (dark) wrestler lifts a knee close to his head, the top (light) man spins to that side and captures a cradle.

Coaching Points: You must teach your wrestlers the top man phrase "head to knee—that's for me." Each time the bottom man puts his head near his knee, have the top man sing the phrase as he captures a cradle.

5.13 CRADLE CONFIDENCE DRILL

Skill Level:
Peewee, junior high, senior high

Basic Skills:
Position, motion

Purpose:
To develop confidence for using the near-side cradle

Prerequisite:
The wrestlers must be able to apply a near-side cradle.

Procedure: Two wrestlers lock near-side cradles on each other and begin to roll around on the mat. They are allowed to roll for 15 to 30 seconds. The coach then signals for live wrestling to commence. The wrestler who is on top must release his cradle immediately and flatten on top of the defensive wrestler so he will not be rolled to his back.

Coaching Points: Wrestlers who are caught on the bottom when the live wrestling whistle blows should be instructed not to panic. In many cases they will be able to arch and roll the opponent to his back.

5.14 JUMP AND HALF DRILL

Skill Level:
Peewee, junior high, senior high

Basic Skills:
Position, motion

Purpose:
To teach the top man to jump and shoot a half nelson when his opponent has lifted an arm from the mat

Prerequisite:
The wrestlers must be able to apply a half nelson.

A

B

Procedure: The bottom man (dark) lies flat on the mat with the light wrestler covering him. The dark wrestler uses his right hand to push back into the light wrestler to regain his base (Figure A). The light wrestler, immediately upon seeing an opening for a half nelson, jumps to that side and forces dark's arm up with an elbow-on-elbow position (Figure B). In a match situation the light wrestler would use a half nelson to work for the fall, but for drill purposes dark reacts by balling in the opposite direction. This movement causes light to jump to the opposite side and catch dark's elbow with his own elbow. The half nelson would follow.

Coaching Points: This drill teaches the bottom man to react to pressure, at the same time allowing the top man to look for openings to shoot a half nelson. Insist that the top man use his elbow to lift the down man's elbow up in the air before putting in a half nelson.

5.15 CROSS FACE CRADLE AND TURK DRILL

Skill Level:
Junior high, senior high, college

Basic Skills:
Position, motion

Purpose:
To teach the top man to react with a cross face cradle or turk for a near fall depending upon the bottom man's reaction

Prerequisite:
The wrestlers must be able to perform a cross face cradle and a turk maneuver.

A

B

C

Procedure: The dark wrestler is broken down into a position flat on the mat. The light wrestler then applies a cross-face with his left hand and a block behind the knee with his right hand in an attempt to apply a cross face cradle (Figure A). The bottom man meanwhile reacts to the pressure by turning into the top man. This causes the top man to release the knee block and pick up the near knee with his right hand (Figure B). The light wrestler then steps in and scores with a turk (Figure C). For drilling purposes only, the light wrestler then releases the turk, allowing the dark wrestler to turn away. This reaction by the dark wrestler causes the light wrestler to apply and score with a cross face cradle.

Coaching Points: Make your wrestlers aware that whichever direction the bottom man turns, the top man should be able to score back points.

5.16 LIFT OR SCREW DRILL

Skill Level:
Junior high, senior high, college

Purpose:
To return a man to the mat from the rear standing position

Basic Skills:
Position, motion, lifting, level change

Prerequisite:
The wrestlers must be able to perform basic lifts and the screw-down maneuver.

Procedure: This drill is a contest to see how many times the light wrestler can either lift the dark wrestler off the mat or screw him down into a takedown position. The rear standing man scores a point each time he completes a successful lift or takedown using the screwdown maneuver. The winner of this contest is the wrestler who scores the most points in a given time period. The screwdown is completed from the rear standing position by putting pressure on the quadriceps muscles with one's elbow. The bottom man must go down to a position where at least one knee is on the mat.

Coaching Points: In today's wrestling, the top man must be taught to bring the bottom man to the mat immediately, otherwise he may be penalized for stalling. If there are no takedowns or lifts scored in a 30-second time period, you might wish to penalize the top man one point.

5.17 STANDING RIDE CONTEST

Skill Level:
Peewee, junior high, senior high

Basic Skills:
Position, motion

Purpose:
To maintain control of a wrestler from the rear standing position without locking hands

Prerequisite:
The wrestlers should have basic knowledge of the hand control concept.

Procedure: The wrestlers assume a stand-up–rear standing position. The top man is not allowed to lock his hands but must attempt to maintain control for a certain time period. The bottom man attempts to score escapes using hand control. Roles are reversed for the next time period. The winner is the one who scores the most escapes.

Coaching Points: This is a good drill to simulate the final seconds of a match. The top man must maintain control to win.

5.18 CROSS DRILL

Skill Level:
Peewee, junior high, senior high, college

Purpose:
To teach wrestlers how to fight off their backs and avoid being pinned

Basic Skills:
Position, motion

Prerequisite:
Each wrestler must be able to perform a back bridge with an opponent on his chest.

Procedure: The light wrestler lies flat on his back with the dark wrestler lying perpendicularly across his chest. The two bodies form a cross. In a live situation, the top wrestler attempts to use a half nelson and crotch combinations to pin while the light wrestler bridges and attempts to clear an arm and get belly-down. In a passive situation, the wrestlers are shown how to bridge and clear an arm between their bodies in defense of a half nelson.

Coaching Points: Be sure your wrestlers understand that to fight off one's back, one must get an arm through between oneself and the opponent's body. Many wrestlers attempt to turn belly-down, but they cannot because their opponents keep them down by blocking the arm.

5.19 LEG–HIP ACTION DRILL

Skill Level:
Peewee, junior high

Basic Skills:
Position, motion

Purpose:
To teach wrestlers proper hip and back positions when attempting to use legs

Prerequisite:
None

Procedure: A wrestler lies on the mat with his weight on his forearms and knees and with his legs crossed. This resembles a seal-walk position. He then practices a right-leg high-leg over to one side, then a left-leg high-leg over to the other side. To simulate an actual wrestling situation, the wrestler must at all times have his back arched to create proper hip pressure.

Coaching Points: This drill should then be done in partners. Determine the proper finish for the head and arm area.

5.20 MOUNT THE BULL CONTEST

Skill Level:
Peewee, junior high, senior high

Basic Skills:
Position, motion

Purpose:
To develop skills needed to put legs on an opponent

Prerequisite:
The wrestlers should be able to put legs on a partner in a drill situation.

Procedure: Wrestlers start in the up–down hover position, with one wrestler on his hands and knees and his partner standing behind him. The bottom man is the bull and the top man is the cowboy. The object of this game is for the cowboy to mount the bull by using an ankle pick and putting his front leg in for a grapevine ride. This enhances the concept of using a far-ankle pick to put in legs. The bull attempts to run on his hands and knees to the opposite wall without being mounted.

Coaching Points: Do not allow the top men to use tackle maneuvers to mount. Insist that they use far-ankle picks with a leg going in to simulate an actual wrestling situation.

5.21 HELICOPTER LEG DRILL

Skill Level:
Junior high, senior high

Basic Skills:
Position, motion

Purpose:
To use leg maneuvers to put an opponent into a near-fall position

Prerequisite:
The wrestlers should have basic knowledge of various leg maneuvers used to score near-fall points.

Procedure: The dark wrestler lies belly-down with his arms folded underneath his chest area. His hands lock on his own elbows. The top man starts with his legs in a cross-body ride position. The object is for the top wrestler to turn the bottom man past a 90-degree angle. The top man scores a point each time a tilt is scored. The roles are then reversed. The winner is the one who scores the most points in a given time period. In most cases, the top man uses a hip-over maneuver to get the bottom man over into the 90-degree position.

Coaching Points: Make sure that the bottom man locks his own elbows under his chest; he is not allowed to use his hands to defend.

CHAPTER 6

BOTTOM MAN DRILLS

This chapter's drills will enhance a wrestler's ability to perform skills needed for executing successful escapes or reversals from the bottom referee's position in the traditional American folkstyle wrestling forum. The basic skills needed for success in the bottom position in folkstyle wrestling are not nearly as well defined as are the basic skills needed to successfully compete from the neutral position. It seems that the original seven basic skills identified by USA Wrestling have been designed to develop skills that enhance the performance of takedowns, the rationale being that the better the wrestlers perform on their feet, the better they perform in international competitions.

Thus there must be some preliminary discussion of the four basic skills needed in the down position. The definitions of these skills differ slightly from the definitions of those same skills as performed in the neutral position. Position, for instance, is defined as keeping arms tight to the sides, keeping forearms extended forward when broken down on the mat, and constantly reacting toward pressure from the top man. Motion will be created by continually executing move after move ("chaining moves"). Chaining should probably be considered a basic skill needed for success from the bottom. Examples of chain wrestling include the stand–switch and the sit-out–roll combinations. The basic skill of level change is used for such maneuvers as the stand-up, the Granby, and combinations of those maneuvers.

The final basic defensive skill is hand control: At all times the down wrestler must have control of one of the offensive wrestler's hands. This should severely limit the attacks the offensive man may employ. However, there is some feeling in the college arena that hand control as a skill is being replaced by the defensive ability to simply "seal off" or assume a safe position by keeping elbows tight to the sides. The claim is that college wrestlers are becoming so proficient with tilts that a failed hand-control attempt may result in a two-point tilt for the opponent. Coaches must make their own decisions regarding the use of hand control as a basic skill of down wrestling.

The basic drills in this chapter include lead-up activities for sits, stand-ups, switches, and shoulder rolls and conclude with a series of chain wrestling activities such as floating (which incorporates chain wrestling by the bottom man and reaction wrestling by the offensive [top] man).

6.1 CHANGEOVER DRILL

Skill Level:
Peewee, junior high, senior high, college

Purpose:
To force the wrestler in the advantage position to change his position of attack

Basic Skills:
Position, motion

Prerequisite:
The wrestlers must be able to assume an up–down referee's position.

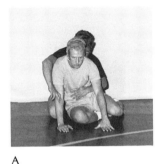

A

B

C

Procedure: This drill may be executed alone or with a partner. Here it will be described as executed with a partner to show dark's position change. The wrestlers begin in referee's position with dark on top and aligned on the "wrong side." The bottom (light) wrestler shifts his legs away from dark in a windshield-wiper-like motion and begins to sit back (Figure A). Light then lifts his hands from the mat and lets them pass in front of his face (Figure B). He continues this motion until his hands are placed back on the mat, bringing himself into a referee's position. The dark wrestler, in the advantage position, has now been forced to attack from the opposite side, thus allowing the light wrestler to work more comfortably for an escape or reversal (Figure C).

Coaching Points: This maneuver is beneficial for any wrestler who feels uncomfortable wrestling an opponent who rides from the "wrong side." Encourage your wrestlers to execute a reversal or escape immediately following the changeover.

6.2 CAT DRILL

Skill Level:
Peewee, junior high

Basic Skill:
Position

Purpose:
To condition a wrestler to fall to the mat in a belly-up position rather than falling to his back, in a potential pinning situation

Prerequisite:
None

Procedure: If you imagine a cat being dropped from an upside-down position, you can immediately visualize the Cat Drill. The cat will always right itself and land in an upright position on it's feet. The wrestler must learn to react in much the same manner. He must develop a sense of time-space and its relationship to the mat. For instance, a wrestler who is being taken down must learn to go "belly down" into a safe position rather than fall to his back, surrendering additional back points. The figure shows the light wrestler holding his hands underneath dark's head in a position that prevents him from falling to the mat. Light at some point releases dark, allowing him to fall to the mat. Dark must react like a cat, righting himself into a referee's position on all fours, or at least into a belly-down position, before he hits the mat. This drill should help wrestlers learn that they must never fall to their backs.

Coaching Points: As the wrestlers become more proficient at this drill, you may want to increase the difficulty level by having the holder push down on the forehead of his partner.

6.3 ROCK OF GIBRALTAR DRILL

Skill Level:
Peewee, junior high, senior high

Basic Skill:
Position

Purpose:
To maintain a base while wrestling from the down position

Prerequisite:
The wrestlers must be able to assume an up–down referee's position.

Procedure: The wrestlers assume an up–down referee's position. The top (advantage) wrestler attempts to break down the bottom wrestler by forcing his hips to the mat. The top wrestler may use various types of attacks—ankle picks, chops, spirals, and so on. The down wrestler attempts to maintain his base. He is allowed to counter only by using hand control, weight transfer, and changeovers.

Coaching Points: Stress that a wrestler must react into pressure or he will have a hard time maintaining his base during competition.

6.4 TENNIS BALL–HAND CONTROL DRILL

Skill Level:

Peewee, junior high

Purpose:

To develop hand control for the bottom wrestler

Basic Skills:

Position, motion, (subskills— chaining, hand control)

Prerequisite:

The bottom wrestler must be able to perform the basic maneuvers in this drill, such as sit-outs, stand-ups, rolls, and switches.

Procedure:

Floating. The top man puts a tennis ball in the hand he would put on his belly button when he is in referee's position. The bottom man then completes a series of moves (sit-outs, stand-ups, etc.) while attempting to hold on to the hand with the ball. This drill is meant to teach the bottom man the concept of hand control.

Sit and Granby Drills. This drill is similar to floating in the previous Tennis Ball Drill except that the bottom man attempts to control the hand with the ball while drilling the sit-back and Granby series.

Coaching Points: This drill can be used two or three times a year to break up the monotony of regular practice sessions. It is especially effective for teaching the hand control concept to beginning or novice wrestlers.

6.5 FROG-ON-FLY HAND CONTROL DRILL

Skill Level:
Peewee, junior high

Basic Skill:
Position, (subskill—hand control)

Purpose:
To obtain hand control when performing a stand-up maneuver

Prerequisite:
The wrestlers must be able to assume a bottom man referee's position.

Procedure: The wrestlers begin this drill in a normal up–down referee's position. The wrestlers are told that the top man's hand on the elbow is a fly. The down man's right hand is a frog. The light wrestler (down man) pushes off the mat using only his hands and a back-arching motion. He tries to slap his right shoulder with his left arm while pretending that his right hand forms a frog's mouth and will slide across to eat the fly. Once the wrestlers grasp the concept of hand control, the drill can be expanded to include a stand-up.

Coaching Points: Once the frog has eaten the fly, instruct the kids to get two-on-one hand control. Then repeat the step until hand control becomes an automatic reaction.

6.6 HAND-FIGHTING HAND CONTROL DRILL

Skill Level:
Peewee, junior high, senior high, college

Basic Skills:
Position, motion, level change, (subskill—hand control)

Purpose:
To obtain hand control from the stand-up position

Prerequisite:
The wrestlers should have been exposed to Drill 6.5.

A

B

Procedure: The light wrestler assumes a stand-up position with his left elbow in a V position tight to his hip and his right hand open but covering the dark wrestler's hand that is on his navel (Figure A). The light wrestler's hips should also be arched away to create pressure on the opponent. The dark wrestler is in a rear standing position with his hands in the same position as if he were in top referee's position.

The actual drill begins on a whistle command, with the dark wrestler attempting to lock hands around the light wrestler's waist. The light wrestler attempts to block off and gain a two-on-one hand control (Figure B). Normally the light wrestler attacks the hand that was on his elbow in the referee's position because he can easily catch it coming across his stomach.

Coaching Points: Once the bottom man develops hand control, you might wish to give the top man another option. Allow the top man to let the light wrestler fall to the mat or to chin him to the mat. This action will force the light wrestler to use the Cat Drill (Drill 6.2) to belly-down and prevent being "stuck" on his back.

6.7 HAND-FIGHTING SEAL-OFF DRILL

Skill Level:
Peewee, junior high, senior high, college

Purpose:
To form a "seal off" position during a stand-up

Basic Skills:
Position, motion, level change

Prerequisite:
The wrestlers must be able to perform a stand-up.

Procedure: This drill differs from the preceding hand control drill only in that the bottom man attempts to seal off with his elbows and forearms, thus preventing the top man from locking around the waist. The coach may want the bottom man to finish this drill with a hip-heist cutoff maneuver.

Coaching Points: Wrestlers should be made to work from this laid-back, arching position so that they learn to react to the movements of the top man. In fact, you may wish to have the rear standing wrestler on his hands and knees.

6.8 STAND-UP JACK DRILL

Skill Level:
Peewee, junior high, senior high, college

Basic Skills:
Position, motion, (subskill—hand control)

Purpose:
To develop the explosive power of the hips and back needed to begin a stand-up

Prerequisite:
The wrestlers must be able to assume a down referee's position.

Procedure: This is an individual drill in which wrestlers practice explosion from the bottom referee's position. The wrestler slaps his right shoulder with his left hand as he arches his back in an attempt to look at the wall behind him. His right hand meanwhile is reaching across his own belly button in an attempt to grab an opponent's wrist for hand control (see Drill 6.5). The momentum of the back slap and arch should bring the wrestler's knees off the mat at least 6 to 12 inches.

Coaching Points: You may wish to use this drill to develop explosive power before teaching Drill 6.5.

6.9 RESISTANCE JACK DRILL

Skill Level:
Junior high, senior high, college

Basic Skills:
Position, motion

Purpose:
To add additional resistance to the back and neck areas for execution of the jack drills

Prerequisite:
The wrestlers should participate in the Stand-Up Jack Drill (Drill 6.8) before adding additional resistance.

A

B

Procedure: There are sandbags commercially available for this type of activity. The coach gives a whistle command, and the sandbag must be thrown off by explosive arching motion (Figure A). Another type of resistance drill uses the wrestling partner to lie across the neck and shoulder areas of the bottom man. The bottom man then jacks up, throwing off the top man (Figure B). This portion of the drill is cost-free, offers much more resistance than the preceding portion, and can save time.

Coaching Points: Insist that the top man must not jump off the bottom man but rather must place his full weight on him for this drill. Sandbags might be more useful for the younger, less physically mature athletes.

6.10 WALL STAND DRILL

Skill Level:
Peewee, junior high, senior high, college

Basic Skills:
Position, motion, (subskills—chaining, hand control)

Purpose:
To practice the steps of a stand-up without a partner

Prerequisite:
The wrestlers should have participated in the jack drills (Drills 6.8 and 6.9).

Procedure: The wrestler assumes a referee's position beside a wall. The wall acts as his opponent. This drill is the same as Drill 6.8 except the wrestler completes the stand-up. The wrestler steps up with his inside foot (the foot closest to the wall) and pivots away from the wall. The pivot action creates back pressure on the wall. The hips are well away from the wall.

Coaching Points: You may want the wrestlers to stop in the wall-stand position to check for proper hip position and hand control. Or you might have the wrestlers do a hip heist to finish the stand-up.

6.11 SANTA'S STUCK IN THE CHIMNEY DRILL

Skill Level:

Peewee, junior high

Basic Skills:

Position, motion, level change

Purpose:

To practice lowering the shoulders through an opponent's grasp

Prerequisite:

None

Procedure: The light wrestler stands behind the dark wrestler with his arms circling dark's chest area. The dark wrestler has his hands up in the air, as if he were Santa Claus sliding down the chimney. The light wrestler tightens his grip, forcing Santa to get stuck. This forces the dark wrestler to dip his shoulder and squirm down through the light wrestler's grip, just as Santa would have to do if he were stuck in the chimney.

Coaching Points: Tell the wrestlers that this is a simple "squirm drill."

6.12 ALL-FOURS HIP HEIST DRILL

Skill Level:
Peewee, junior high, senior high, college

Purpose:
To practice the skill of a "low-leg under" or hip heist

Basic Skills:
Position, motion

Prerequisite:
None

A

B

C

D

Procedure: A wrestler begins in a belly-up crab position (Figure A) with his weight supported on his hands and feet. He crosses his left leg underneath his right leg (Figure B). This maneuver positions him into a belly-down-on-all-fours position (Figure C), much the same as that of a defensive lineman. The wrestler then crosses his right leg underneath his left leg (Figure D), returning him to crab position.

Coaching Points: Do not allow the wrestlers to sit on their buttocks during this drill.

6.13 (LONG SIT-OUT) HIP HEIST DRILL

Skill Level:
Peewee, junior high, senior high, college

Basic Skills:
Position, motion, (subskill—chaining)

Purpose:
To incorporate the hip heist skill into an actual wrestling maneuver such as the long sit-out

Prerequisite:
The wrestlers should be able to perform a hip heist and a sit-out.

Procedure: The wrestler completes a long sit-out and crosses his right leg under his left leg to finish.

Coaching Points: This is an exceptional way to drill long sit-outs because in a match situation most wrestlers expect the defensive man to turn the opposite way in an attempt to roll or come out the back door.

6.14 WALL SIT–HIP HEIST DRILL

Skill Level:
Peewee, junior high, senior high

Purpose:
To incorporate the hip heist as a finish for the stand-up maneuver

Basic Skills:
Position, motion, level change, back arch, (subskill—chaining)

Prerequisite:
The wrestlers must be able to perform a hip heist and a stand-up.

Procedure: The wrestler sits on the floor with his back to the wall. On a whistle command, he arches back against the wall (in a motion similar to the forceback used in a stand-up) and executes a long sit-out to a hip heist. See Drill 6.12 for proper execution of a hip heist.

Coaching Points: This drill combines the ingredients of the sit-back, stand-up, and hip heist into one drill. It should have effective carryover value for match situations.

6.15 WINDSHIELD WIPER SITS DRILL

Skill Level:
Peewee, junior high

Basic Skills:
Position, motion

Purpose:
To clear the legs to one side before performing a sit-back maneuver

Prerequisite:
The wrestlers should be able to assume a down referee's position.

Procedure: The wrestlers assume down referee's positions without partners. On command, each wrestler sits his legs and feet to the side that would be away from an imaginary partner. This action resembles that of a windshield wiper. In fact, have the wrestlers pretend that their legs are windshield wipers and wipe them back and forth on the mat. After they get the feel of the windshield wiper motion, have them use their hands to push back into a sit position.

Coaching Points: The key to this maneuver is encouraging the wrestlers to use their legs to move in a windshield wiper–type motion in order to clear them away from an opponent's attack.

6.16 BRIDGE-AROUND–HIGH LEG DRILL

Skill Level:
Junior high, senior high, college

Basic Skills:
Position, motion

Purpose:
To be used as a lead-up for the tripod sit-out, and to enhance a wrestler's ability to execute a high-leg over maneuver from a bridging situation. This drill is used by the Soviets as a skill test for prospective elite wrestling candidates.

Prerequisite:
The wrestlers must be able to perform a high-leg maneuver and a front and back bridge.

A

B

C

Procedure: This drill begins with a wrestler in a front bridge position. His hands are locked with a finger-chain grip in front of his face, and his elbows are flat on the mat (Figure A). He begins to walk on his feet, rotating his body in a counterclockwise motion and maintaining the flat elbow position. He rotates until he reaches a point at which the flat elbow position cannot be maintained unless a high-leg over is performed. The wrestler takes his left foot and steps over his right leg (Figure B). The high-leg maneuver positions him in a back bridge. The circular rotation continues until the flat elbow position once again cannot be maintained. At this point, the wrestler kicks his right foot over his left leg, returning to the front bridge position (Figure C). (This movement is similar to kicking a soccer ball in upside-down "Pelé style.") This concludes one full rotation for the bridge-around. The drill must be completed slowly at first; rotation speed is emphasized after technique and flexibility improve.

Coaching Points: Initially, wrestlers will want to raise their elbows off the mat. Insist that they maintain the flat elbow position during rotation, to obtain maximum flexibility.

6.17 SIT-OUT AND ROLL-EVEN DRILL

Skill Level:
Peewee, junior high, senior high

Purpose:
To create a chaining action with a series of sit-outs

Basic Skills:
Position, motion, (subskill—chaining)

Prerequisite:
Wrestlers must be able to perform a long sit-out.

Procedure: Each wrestler works without a partner, starting from a down referee's position. On a whistle command, the wrestler completes a long sit-out to one side, followed by another long sit-out to the opposite side. The routine continues for a given time period.

Coaching Points: Encourage your wrestlers to move as fast as possible and not to hesitate between moves. This drill can be used as part of a cardiovascular circuit workout such as PTA (Drill 8.4). It is also a good exercise to use to practice floating (Drill 5.6).

6.18 GET-PERPENDICULAR CONTEST

Skill Level:
Junior high, senior high, college

Basic Skills:
Position, hand control

Purpose:
To avoid being tilted by the top man

Prerequisite:
The top man must be able to execute a tilt.

Procedure: The wrestlers start in an up–down referee's position. The top man attempts to tilt the bottom man, exposing his back to a 90-degree position, with a near arm–tight waist combination. The top man scores a point each time he accomplishes the 90-degree tilt. The bottom man attempts to get into a position perpendicular to the top man to avoid the tilt. The roles are reversed for the next time period.

Coaching Points: Insist that your wrestlers learn how to get themselves into a perpendicular position to avoid being tilted.

6.19 SHOULDER ROLL DRILL

Skill Level:
Peewee, junior high

Basic Skills:
Position, motion

Purpose:
To begin development of a shoulder roll

Prerequisite:
None

Procedure:

1. The wrestler sits on a crease of the mat. He rolls to his left shoulder and pretends he is kicking a soccer ball with his right foot. This motion should bring him into a shoulder–shoulder position on the mat, and momentum brings him through to a sitting position. He should still be sitting on the crease of the mat, facing the same direction as when he started.

2. The wrestler sits on the mat, placing his hands on his hips. He rolls to the side, supporting himself with his neck, shoulders, and elbows.

Coaching Points: This is a good exercise to use to warm up the neck muscles before practice or live wrestling.

6.20 FLIP GRANBY DRILL

Skill Level:
Peewee, junior high, senior high, college

Purpose:
To be used as a lead-up for a flip Granby maneuver

Basic Skills:
Position, motion, level change

Prerequisite:
Wrestlers should be able to perform a basic shoulder roll.

A   B

Procedure: The emphasis for executing a flip Granby is to get the hips in an elevated position and kick a leg over one's head. This drill shows wrestlers how to accomplish that. The down wrestler takes his left foot and steps it into a position in front of his right knee. He then steps his right foot behind the heel of the left foot. The hips are high off the mat (Figure A). The second phase is to kick the right leg straight up into a handstand-type position (Figure B). The wrestler completes the flip motion by tucking his head and throwing his left arm through and past his right knee.

Coaching Points: Insist that your wrestlers have their hips elevated. Have your wrestlers practice the first stage several times before performing the actual flip.

Author's Note: The Granby system of wrestling seems to be a complete school of wrestling within itself. Therefore, coaches interested in developing a Granby system are advised to attend the Granby School of Wrestling in Virginia. For more information contact: Granby School of Wrestling, P.O. Box 7127, Back Bay Station, Virginia Beach, Virginia 23457.

6.21 STANDING FLIP GRANBY DRILL

Skill Level:
Peewee, junior high, senior high, college

Purpose:
To execute an aerial flip Granby from the stand-up position

Basic Skills:
Position, motion, level change

Prerequisite:
Wrestlers should be able to perform a simple cartwheel (one-handed) and a basic shoulder roll.

Procedure: The aerial flip Granby is simply a shoulder roll that is begun from the standing position. The wrestler takes two steps to the right, stops, changes direction by tucking his left shoulder, and flips in a shoulder-roll motion. The wrestler should practice the drill in three phases: using (if he wants to) his left hand to cartwheel when completing the flip, then completing the drill by himself, and then completing the flip Granby with a partner.

Coaching Points: Be sure your wrestlers practice a simple shoulder roll and a regular flip Granby before they try an aerial Granby.

SAFETY CONCERNS

It is advisable to use a spotter when a wrestler is first attempting this skill. This would help insure that the wrestler not fall on his head and damage muscles in his neck.

6.22 CONCEDE TAKEDOWN DRILL

Skill Level:
Junior high, senior high, college

Purpose:
To make wrestlers realize that there are times when a takedown must be conceded in order to come to the mat in a "safe" position, preparing to score an immediate reversal

Basic Skills:
Position, motion, level change, (subskill—hand control)

Prerequisite:
The wrestlers must be able to perform a single leg takedown and a wrist roll.

Procedure: The dark wrestler begins this drill by capturing a single leg on the light wrestler. The dark wrestler is instructed to score a takedown finish; the light wrestler is instructed to concede "at a point of no return." As the light wrestler concedes, he falls to a safe position on his knees with one hand near his side or belly button. This maneuver should bait dark to put his arm around light's waist and grab the hand that is on the belly button. This allows light to overcontrol dark's hand with his opposite hand and execute a cross-arm wrist roll. If the roll is not effective or if the top man does not control the hand around the waist, the light wrestler is at least in a safe position.

Coaching Points: Instruct your wrestlers to recognize when to give up a takedown and when to keep fighting off an attack. It is much more advantageous to give up a two-point takedown with the possibility of an immediate reversal than it is to give up five points and be fighting off one's back.

6.23 SWITCH–ELEVATOR DRILL

Skill Level:
Junior high, senior high

Purpose:
To effectively score against an opponent who steps over a leg in an attempt to stop a switch maneuver

Basic Skills:
Position, motion, (subskill—chaining)

Prerequisite:
The wrestlers must be able to perform a basic switch and an elevator maneuver.

A   B

Procedure: The light wrestler executes a switch, and dark counters by stepping over and between light's legs (Figure A). The dark wrestler has his head down and hips up in the air. Light kicks up through dark's crotch, lifting dark's hips and forcing him into a somersault. When first attempting this maneuver, the wrestler should elevate his opponent several times without kicking him over into a somersault. Once this skill has been learned, light elevates and uses his right calf to catch behind dark's knee. The movements of dark's somersault (Figure B) pull light over on top. Light then scrambles for a near fall with any catch-as-catch-can maneuver.

Coaching Points: The end of this drill can be particularly useful in teaching wrestlers how to scramble in a catch-as-catch-can situation. Caution wrestlers against lying on or nearly on their backs for an extended period while attempting to elevate, because some referees will count back points.

6.24 SWITCH AND RESWITCH CHAINS DRILL

Skill Level:
Peewee, junior high, senior high, college

Basic Skills:
Position, motion, (subskill—chaining)

Purpose:
To practice the switch, and switch counter, in a chaining situation

Prerequisite:
The wrestlers must be able to perform all components of the chain: outside-leg reswitch, inside-leg reswitch, hip heist, and bear crawl.

Procedure:

Switch–Outside-Leg Reswitch. The light wrestler executes a switch. The dark wrestler counters by lifting his leg and sitting away from the light wrestler (Figure A). The wrestlers continue the switch–reswitch routine.

A

Switch–Reswitch–Roll Chain. The light wrestler executes a switch, and dark counters by sitting to the outside for a reswitch. Dark thinks he has successfully countered light's switch attempt. As dark begins to come up top to maintain control, light uses his right elbow to lock onto dark's elbow, does a right-shoulder dive (Figure B), and then hips over for the score (Figures C and D).

B

C

D

Switch–Inside-Leg Reswitch. This drill is the same as the switch–outside-leg reswitch except the reswitch man (the dark wrestler) sits underneath and into his opponent (Figure E). Many wrestlers use this method even though it can be easily countered by a hip heist–bear crawl. The wrestlers continue a switch–reswitch routine.

E

Switch–Inside Reswitch–Hip Heist–Bear Crawl Chain. This drill carries the last drill one step further. The inside-leg reswitch is countered by the light wrestler executing a right-leg heist (Figure F) and then using a bear crawl toward the head, picking up a half nelson and crotch body press (Figure G).

F   G

Coaching Points: This switch series of reaction drills can also be incorporated into a floating exercise.

6.25 SIT-BACK REACTION DRILL

Skill Level:

Junior high, senior high, college

Purpose:

To teach a wrestler the proper method of scoring from the sit-back position depending upon the top man's actions

Basic Skills:

Position, motion, level change, (subskills—chaining, hand control)

Prerequisite:

The wrestlers should be able to perform the reactions involved in this drill.

Procedure: The bottom man does a sit-back into his partner while maintaining control of the hand on his belly button. The coach then designates the movement the top man should use to stop the sit-back. The bottom man then uses that movement to score. A series of action–reaction situations might include the following:

Top man action	*Bottom reaction for score*
1. Hang arm over shoulder	Fan out to side
2. Hang head over shoulder	Fan and catch head
3. Near-arm chop	Shoulder roll or tripod
4. Near-arm chop follow-around	Tripod to Peterson roll
5. Force pressure into back	Stand-up
6. Chin back	Scoot back to maintain base
7. Arm bar	Hand control and arm drag

Coaching Points: You may want to design a different system for reaction to the top man and drill it so that it will become automatic when the situations occur.

6.26 BLINDFOLD DRILL

Skill Level:
Peewee, junior high, senior high

Purpose:
To develop a kinesthetic awareness of wrestling movements

Basic Skills:
Position, motion, (subskills—
chaining, hand control)

Prerequisite:
The wrestlers should be able to
perform basic top and bottom
man maneuvers.

Procedure: The down wrestler is blindfolded and instructed to execute various wrestling skills. This situation can include live wrestling as long as contact is maintained between wrestlers.

Coaching Points: The blindfold situation can also be used for wrestlers in the neutral position. However, the blind-start position should
be used, and wrestlers must maintain contact throughout the drill.

SAFETY CONCERNS

Insist that once contact between wrestlers has broken, all
combat must stop. Blind wrestling from a noncontact position could lead to potential injury.

CHAPTER 7

GAMES
AND MAT-RELATED
ACTIVITIES

This chapter contains many games and other activities that can be played on a wrestling mat and will give peewee and junior high school wrestlers a great deal of emotional and physical pleasure. Even the most advanced high school wrestler will find most of these to be a welcome relief from the normal rigors of daily training. The physical educator would be able to use many of them for a basic combative class.

The activities fall into three major categories: (a) individual or dual wrestling-related contests, such as Sumo Wrestling, featuring one-on-one competition using the basic skills of wrestling; (b) team wrestling contests, such as Rodeo, involving team-concept competition using basic wrestling skills; and (c) activities that have been modified to be played on a wrestling mat, such as Knee Football. Although these types of activities don't teach new wrestling skills, they do give wrestlers relaxing and enjoyable diversions from the more rigorous aspects of daily practice.

For these drills, the Basic Skills section often reads "N/A" ("not applicable"). This is because many of the activities do not teach basic wrestling skills. However, they can still be an important part of any wrestling program.

Peewee and junior high school programs must provide a "fun-type" atmosphere, and wrestling-related games are one way to do that. The activities in this chapter can be used to promote the sport of wrestling and hopefully to recruit future participants. Wrestlers at the higher levels will find them a welcome addition to their normal regime of daily training. All of these activities can be revised to meet the needs of your program.

7.1 BODY CRAWL

Skill Level:
Junior high, senior high, college

Basic Skills:
N/A

Purpose:
To cling and climb on and around another person's body

Prerequisite:
None

Procedure: The light wrestler stands on the mat with his arms bent at the elbows and his forearms extending forward. The dark wrestler jumps on the waist of the light wrestler. The objective is for the dark wrestler to crawl up and over the light wrestler's head and shoulders, down his back, through his crotch, and back to the starting position. He must do this without touching the mat with any part of his body.

Coaching Points: The toughest phase of this exercise is getting the legs through the crotch area without touching the mat. In most cases the foundation man should be slightly larger than his partner due to the strength needed for maintaining a solid base. This skill can be used as a game to see who can actually execute the skill, or it can be a contest of speed.

7.2 KNEE COMBAT CONTEST

Skill Level:

Peewee, junior high, senior high

Purpose:

This contest is designed to practice skills used when wrestling a man who is on both knees in the neutral position

Basic Skills:

Position, motion, level change, penetration

Prerequisite:

The wrestlers should possess the competence to perform basic scoring maneuvers from the neutral position.

Procedure: One wrestler must stay on both knees and defend himself from being taken down. He may not step up with a foot for balance. The other wrestler uses any takedown available to score. The roles are then reversed. Whoever scores the most takedowns in a certain time period is the winner.

Coaching Points: Wrestlers will have the most success by using a series of snaps, shucks, and shrug maneuvers to score.

7.3 CHIN AND HEAD DUCK CONTEST

Skill Level:
Junior high, senior high, college

Basic Skills:
Position, penetration, lifting

Purpose:
To use head rotation and a "looking up" motion when using a duckunder

Prerequisite:
The wrestlers should be able to perform a dunkunder manuever from the neutral position.

Procedure: The wrestlers both use their right hands to go over each other's neck and hold onto their partner's chin. They are both on their knees. The contest is to see who can put the other to his back first, using this grip and head position. Each wrestler may let one knee come off the mat and use a foot for support.

Coaching Points: Caution your wrestlers not to use a neck wrench when grabbing the chin. They may use only head and neck rotation to score.

7.4 SQUAT BACK WRESTLING

Skill Level:
Peewee, junior high, senior high

Purpose:
To engage in a "scramble wrestling" situation

Basic Skills:
Position, motion, level change, penetration, lifting, backstep, and back arch

Prerequisite:
The wrestlers should be able to perform basic wrestling maneuvers.

Procedure: The wrestlers assume a back-to-back squat position. They must be leaning against each other to stay on their feet. On the whistle, live wrestling occurs.

Coaching Points: This is another game that is useful both in physical education class and as a scramble wrestling situation in the practice room. Encourage the wrestlers to score immediately after facing one another.

7.5 SUMO WRESTLING

Skill Level:
Peewee, junior high, senior high, college

Purpose:
To engage in a takedown contest within a confined area. This contest contains a sumo wrestling element because the contest can be won by throwing the opponent from the circle.

Basic Skills:
Position, motion, level change, penetration, lifting, backstep, back arch

Prerequisite:
The wrestlers should have a basic competence in performing neutral-position scoring maneuvers.

Procedure: Two wrestlers face off in a 10-foot circle. The objective is to push each other out of the circle or to score a takedown inside the circle. The first wrestler to touch outside the circle is the loser unless a takedown has been scored. Many times a wrestler who is being pushed out will use a lateral drop or headlock to score and end up the winner.

Coaching Points: This can be used to match individual wrestling skills, and it is no more dangerous than in any other combative exercise.

7.6 LOG ROLL GAME

Skill Level:
Peewee, junior high

Purpose:
To engage in a scramble wrestling situation

Basic Skills:
Position, motion, level change, lifting, backstep, back arch

Prerequisite:
The wrestlers should possess competence in performing basic scoring maneuvers.

Procedure: Wrestlers lie side by side with a 5-foot space between them. Each wrestler has his head even with the other's feet. The wrestlers are instructed to roll toward each other and to commence live wrestling as soon as they make contact.

Coaching Points: Emphasize that the wrestlers are not to commence live wrestling until contact has been made. This game provides an excellent situation for practicing scramble wrestling. It may also be used as an activity for physical education class.

7.7 DEAD COCKROACH

Skill Level:
Peewee, junior high

Purpose:
To have fun and to engage in a scramble wrestling situation

Basic Skills:
Position, motion, level change, penetration, lifting, backstep, back arch

Prerequisite:
The wrestlers should possess competence in performing basic scoring maneuvers from the up–down referee's position.

Procedure: The game begins with wrestlers lying side by side in the head-to-feet position. They are instructed to imagine themselves as cockroaches. The coach tells them that he is going to spray them with insecticide. As he pretends to do this, they are to act like dying cockroaches—complete with convulsions and trembling limbs. Then on a whistle command they wrestle live. Kids have great fun playing this game.

Coaching Points: This is a great game, but you must give it a great buildup before starting. It can be used in the peewee practice room or in elementary and junior high physical education classes.

7.8 ZONE DRILL

Skill Level:
Junior high, senior high

Purpose:
To keep wrestlers inbounds and out of the zone area in freestyle and Greco-Roman wrestling

Basic Skills:
Position, motion, level change, penetration, lifting, backstep, back arch

Prerequisite:
The wrestlers should be able to maintain a proper stance and create motion.

Procedure:

Freestyle–Greco-Roman Drill. One wrestler is placed with his feet on or near, and his back toward, the out-of-bounds line. On command, the wrestler on the inside attempts to force the other to stay close to the line or go out of bounds. The wrestler with his back to the circle must turn his opponent so that his opponent's back is to the outside. He may use snaps, shucks, or shrugs to turn his opponent.

Folkstyle Drill. In folkstyle wrestling, the offensive wrestler wants his back to the out-of-bounds line so that he may penetrate across the entire mat (if needed) for a score. However, wrestlers are not allowed to "play the edge of the mat."

Coaching Points: This is an excellent drill for preparing wrestlers for freestyle or Greco-Roman competition.

7.9 STEAL THE DRAGON'S TAIL

Skill Level:

Peewee, junior high

Purpose:

To utilize various wrestling techniques needed for a match situation, but in a game-like atmosphere

Basic Skills:

Position, motion, level change, penetration

Prerequisite:

The wrestlers should be able to perform basic scoring maneuvers in the neutral position.

Procedure: The game begins with each wrestler tucking a sock into the back of his wrestling shorts. The sock should hang out at least 6 to 8 inches. The coach then gives a command, such as "The game is to steal the dragon's tail by using a high-crotch maneuver." The wrestler who steals the opponent's sock by executing a high crotch would be the winner. There are other maneuvers that could be used in Steal the Dragon's Tail: arm drags, snapdowns, duckunders, or a free-for-all, for instance.

Coaching Points: Insist that the wrestlers let the socks hang out of their shorts at least 6 inches. Some wrestlers may attempt to tie the sock to their jock to avoid losing the competition. This is unacceptable for the obvious reason.

7.10 SIMON SAYS—WALL SQUAT GAME

Skill Level:
Peewee, junior high

Basic Skills:
N/A

Purpose:
To develop cognitive (thinking and reaction) faculties under physical stress

Prerequisite:
None

Procedure: One wrestler assumes a squat position against a wall on a wrestling mat. His opponent faces him and becomes "Simon" for a 3-minute Simon Says game.

For example, the Simon wrestler will say, "Simon says, 'Touch your left knee with your right hand,'" simultaneously touching his own left knee with right hand. The wrestler on the wall will then perform the proper movement. If the wrestler on the wall makes a movement not described by Simon, his opponent scores one point. The roles are then reversed for another 3-minute time period. The movements Simon picks might include backslaps, hand control, snap motion, drag motion, or tapping of various body parts.

Coaching Points: This game will help to build endurance in the quadriceps muscles of a wrestler and hopefully help him to maintain a proper stance throughout an entire match. The wrestler who scores the most points by fooling his partner should receive some type of a reward after practice. This game can be used to conclude a wrestling practice or for physical education class. While this game is being played you may wish to elaborate on the importance of maintaining a proper stance late in a match.

7.11 BALMERT'S MATOPOLY*

Skill Level:
Junior high, senior high

Purpose:
To provide a break from the daily practice routine, while including many of the wrestling skills and physical exercises of a regular practice

Basic Skills:
Position, motion, level change, penetration, lifting, backstep, back arch

Prerequisite:
The wrestlers should have a basic competence in all wrestling technique maneuvers.

Procedure: This game is played using a normal Monopoly board. A coach must take pieces of tape and relabel, as follows, the board properties, utilities, and railroads, and so on—these will be bought by the wrestlers with exercises instead of money.

Board Space	Cost
Vermont Avenue	20 sit-ups
Connecticut Avenue	25 sit-ups
Oriental Avenue	20 sit-ups
St. Charles Place	25 push-ups
States Avenue	25 push-ups
Virginia Avenue	30 push-ups
Pacific Avenue	25 squat thrusts
North Carolina Avenue	25 squat thrusts
Pennsylvania Avenue	30 squat thrusts
Indiana Avenue	10 pull-ups
Illinois Avenue	12 pull-ups
Kentucky Avenue	10 pull-ups
Marvin Gardens	25 grass drills
Atlantic Avenue	25 grass drills
Ventnor Avenue	30 grass drills
St. James Place	25 squat jumps
Tennessee Avenue	25 squat jumps

(Cont.)

---

*This game is the brainchild of Coach Mickey Balmert of Bishop Ready High School, Columbus, Ohio.

(Continued)

Board Space	Cost
New York Avenue	30 squat jumps
Boardwalk	25 6-count squat thrusts
Park Place	25 6-count squat thrusts
Mediterreanean Avenue	25 mountain climbers
Baltic Avenue	25 mountain climbers
Railroads	3 bear crawls, length of the room
Luxury Tax and Income Tax	20 reverse push-ups
Any utility	Leap frogs (twice the amount on dice throw)
Go	Get free drink
Just visiting jail	10 jumping jacks
In jail	Fight off back

The Chance and Community Chest cards should be labeled with various skills, such as the following:

hit 5 doubles

do 5 duckunders

5 singles to right side

do 5 firearms

get off back 5 bridge and turn

5 butt drags

5 finishes off two-on-one

5 sit-backs

5 high crotches

5 team-assigned drills

5 cradle finishes

5 arm drags

5 ankle picks

single finishes on mat, head inside

5 high halfs

5 single finishes off mat

5 head snaps

5 stand-ups

5 single finishes on head, inside

5 headlocks

The rules are very simple. The wrestlers are divided into two teams, and "coaches" or "captains" roll the dice. Each time a team lands on a property or utility they must pay for it by doing the prescribed exercises; if that team lands on that property again, they can put a house on it for another set of exercises. If a team lands on a property owned by the opponents, they have to do double the prescribed exercises if there are no houses on it, 3 times the exercises for one house, and 4 times the exercises for two houses. A team must land on Go to get a drink. The game should be played 2 hours, with the losing team rolling up the mats or with the winning team getting a refreshment such as fruit or a fruit drink.

Coaching Points: This would be a great game to play using the varsity against the junior varsity. Don't use this game more than once or twice a season, as it might become boring.

7.12 CRADLE-GRIP CIRCLE GAME

Skill Level:
Peewee, junior high, senior high

Basic Skills:
N/A

Purpose:
To improve the grip a wrestler would use to apply a cradle

Prerequisite:
Wrestlers should be able to lock their hands using either a wrestler's grip (cupped hands) or finger-chain grip.

Procedure: Twelve wrestlers sit in a circle with their feet pointing to the inside of the circle. They interlock their arms with the arms of the wrestlers next to them and lock their own hands; this forms a complete chain around the circle. Wrestlers are told to pretend that they have a cradle locked up and that they should attempt to bring their elbows close together to tighten the grip. At this point, the wrestlers lean back and lie on their backs. Any wrestler whose grip is broken is eliminated from the circle and assigned to pummel or spar until the contest concludes. This activity continues until there are only two wrestlers left in the circle. Another way for a wrestler to be eliminated is by being pulled off the mat and onto his feet. This might occur once there are only three wrestlers left in the circle.

Coaching Points: This game is relatively safe at all levels. Most players will break their grip before any injury would occur to shoulders or arms.

7.13 MAT WARS

Skill Level:
Peewee, junior high, senior high

Purpose:
To practice wrestling from the neutral position while upright on one's knees

Basic Skills:
Position, motion, level change, penetration

Prerequisite:
The wrestlers should be able to perform basic wrestling maneuvers.

Procedure: The wrestlers begin the game upright on their knees. The coach blows his whistle to begin the contest, and the wrestlers all attempt to score takedowns. When a wrestler is taken down, he must go to the sidelines. The last wrestler standing is the champion. The contest should be contested in three divisions: lightweight, middleweight, and heavyweight.

Coaching Points: Be cautious about letting lightweight wrestlers compete with heavyweight wrestlers. It is suggested that champions be crowned in each of the three divisions. Advise your wrestlers that all competition must be in one-on-one situations.

7.14 MAT TUG-OF-WAR

Skill Level:
Peewee, junior high

Basic Skills:
N/A

Purpose:
To simply have fun on a wrestling mat

Prerequisite:
None

Procedure: The wrestlers are divided into two teams, separated by a line (usually the line will be where sections of the mat are taped together). All wrestlers must stay on their hands and knees. The object of this game is for members of one team to pull the members of the other team across the line. Once a wrestler has been pulled completely across the line, he must sit against the wall. The wall is "jail" until the game is complete. The rules are very simple: no biting, scratching, or standing up to pull a wrestler across the line. Teammates are not allowed to help each other defend against being pulled across the line.

Coaching Points: Make sure that the wrestlers do not stand up on their feet to pull an opponent.

7.15 COWBOYS AND INDIANS

Skill Level:
Peewee, junior high

Basic Skills:
Position, motion

Purpose:
To practice maintaining a base for the bottom man and riding for the top man

Prerequisite:
None

Procedure: The top men mount up as if they were riders on horses. They must ride in a crab-leg fashion with toes tucked in the horse's (down man's) calves. The contest is to knock other riders off of their horses or to knock the horses off of their bases. The top man (rider) is not allowed to put his feet on the mat to maintain a base. Once the wrestlers are knocked down, they must go to the side of the mat until a winner has been determined. This contest can be individual or in teams such as cowboys and Indians.

Coaching Points: Do not allow wrestlers to put their feet on the mat. Discourage ganging up (several riders against one rider).

7.16 SHARKS AND MINNOWS

Skill Level:
Peewee, junior high

Basic Skills:
Position, motion

Purpose:
To develop upper body movement skills

Prerequisite:
The wrestlers should possess basic knowledge of the wrestling skills needed for this contest.

Procedure: The game begins with four wrestlers in the middle of the wrestling room upright on their knees; they are the "sharks." The rest of the wrestlers line up next to a wall, also on their knees; they are the "minnows." The object of the game is for the minnows to cross the room on their knees without sharks attacking them and exposing their backs to the mat. If the shark attacks a minnow and exposes his back to the mat, that minnow then becomes a shark. The minnows continue crossing the mat until there is only one left. He is the winner.

This game can also be played in teams. A team or "school" of sharks would consist of six wrestlers. In this case, the minnows simply see how many times in a 2-minute period they can cross the mat without having their backs exposed to the mat. In this team version, the exposed wrestlers sit off to the side after they have been exposed. After 2 minutes the next school of sharks goes into the middle. The winning team is decided by how many minnows' backs were exposed in each 2-minute time period.

Coaching Points: You may also change techniques to be used by the sharks; for example, sharks might score only using headlocks, or they might tilt rather than expose backs, to score. This can be a team wrestling game or a physical education activity game.

7.17 RODEO

Skill Level:
Junior high, senior high, college

Basic Skills:
Position, motion

Purpose:
To practice tilting an opponent while having fun in a game-like situation

Prerequisite:
The wrestlers must be able to perform basic tilts from referee's position.

Procedure: Six wrestlers are needed. There are two teams, each consisting of a horse, rider, and bull. Two wrestlers are down on all fours (they are horses), two are riders (they are the cowboys), and another two are down on all fours (they are the bulls). The object of the game is for each team's rider and horse to approach the other team's bull and attempt to bulldog him to the mat. The first rider to jump from his horse onto a bull and successfully bulldog him into a tilt position is the winner.

Coaching Points: This is a good game to play at camp or during a light day at practice. The kids will love it.

7.18 CHICKEN FIGHTING

Skill Level:
Peewee, junior high

Basic Skills:
Position, motion

Purpose:
To develop balance in a competitive setting

Prerequisite:
None

Procedure: The wrestlers are directed to score takedowns while hopping on one foot. Each wrestler must hold one leg up with a hand and use the free hand for combat; using drags, shucks, and shrugs, he tries to knock his opponent from his feet.

Coaching Points: You may wish to allow each wrestler to hop but not hold up his foot. This would allow the wrestlers to use both hands and the free leg to block and trip with. The wrestler would then be able to use foot sweeps and trips for takedowns.

SAFETY CONCERNS

Make sure the contests are properly divided into light-weight, middleweight, and heavyweight classes.

7.19 MAT CHESS

Skill Level:
Peewee, junior high

Basic Skills:
N/A

Purpose:
To have fun on a wrestling mat during a crash course in chess

Prerequisite:
None

Procedure: The game consists of two teams of 16 people each. The teams face each other in the following formation:

Front Line.   Eight wrestlers on their hands and knees. These are the pawns and can go anywhere on the mat as long as they stay on all fours.

Second Line.   Seven wrestlers up-right on their knees. These wrestlers are the bishops, knights, rooks, and queen; they also can go anywhere on the mat as long as they stay on their knees.

Third Line.   One wrestler standing on his feet. He is the king and can go anywhere on the mat.

The object of the game is to capture the opponent's king and bring him to the mat.

Coaching Points: Play the game seven or eight times and encourage the teams to develop strategies for protecting their own king while attempting to capture their opponents' king.

SAFETY CONCERNS
There is a slight risk of kids' falling on each other; however, most will slip away from any danger zone. *Do not allow the king to use a wall to hold himself upright—if he does that, stop play immediately and declare the opposing team winner of that game.*

7.20 CRAB KILLS

Skill Level:
Peewee, junior high

Basic Skills:
N/A

Purpose:
To enhance endurance of the arm muscles while having fun on the wrestling mat

Prerequisite:
None

Procedure: All of the wrestlers in the room are to assume belly-up crab positions with their weight supported on their hands and feet. The object of the game is to force an opposing wrestler to touch his buttocks on the mat, eliminating him. The last wrestler remaining in the crab position is the winner. The wrestlers may trip another wrestler, pull his arms out from under him, or just ram an opponent to force him down on his buttocks.

Coaching Points: The participants must not be allowed to kick during this game. This is an excellent activity for wrestling practice or physical education classes.

7.21 MEDICINE BALL ACTIVITIES

Skill Level:
Junior high, senior high

Basic Skills:
N/A

Purpose:
To have fun on a wrestling mat and possibly develop some muscular endurance

Prerequisite:
None

Procedure:

Wrestle for the Ball. In this game a medicine ball is placed in a circle with two wrestlers. The contest is to see who can control the ball and carry it out of the circle.

Rugby Ball. There are two teams in a room with a medicine ball. The object is to get the ball to one end or the other of the room. The wrestlers must stay on their knees and may only carry, throw, or roll the ball (and may not bite, pinch, scratch, etc.).

Neck Isometrics. This is a simple conditioning drill in which a wrestler puts the ball on the mat and lays his head on it in a belly-up position. He then straightens his body so that only his feet are on the mat. This is an excellent neck exercise. It is best used in a circuit training drill.

Coaching Points: The rugby ball might be better suited for a physical education class, but wrestling for the ball and using the ball for neck isometrics are excellent wrestling-related activities.

7.22 STICK WRESTLING CONTESTS

Skill Level:
Peewee, junior high, senior high, college

Purpose:
To develop muscular strength throughout a desired range of motion during combative exercise

Basic Skills:
N/A

Prerequisite:
None

Procedure:

Right Tip Down. Two wrestlers stand facing each other and holding a stick over their heads. On command, each wrestler attempts to push the end of the stick that's at his left side in an upward motion and the end that's to his right in a downward motion. This same contest could be executed with the stick held at waist or chest level (Figure A).

A

Lift the Partner. Two wrestlers grasp a heavy stick at thigh level. On command, one wrestler attempts to lift the stick over his head while the other opposes. Roles are reversed for the next time session.

Pullover. Two wrestlers stand back to back holding a stick overhead. On command, each wrestler attempts to bring the stick down in front of his chest. This action will pull his opponent over his back (Figure B).

B

Coaching Points: Use a stick that is heavy enough not to break during competition. A shovel or fork handle might serve well for this exercise. These types of activities might be included as a station in circuit training.

7.23 FORCE THE ELBOWS

Skill Level:
Junior high, senior high, college

Basic Skills:
N/A

Purpose:
To be used as isometric exercises to develop strength in the shoulder and arm areas

Prerequisite:
The wrestlers should participate in numerous flexibility exercises before engaging in this contest.

A

B

Procedure: A wrestler locks his hands behind his head and leans against a wall in a squat position. His elbows are pointing toward his partner, who is standing directly in front of him (Figure A). The contest is to see how long it takes the partner to push the squatting wrestler's elbows against the mat on the wall (Figure B).

Coaching Points: Instruct your wrestlers to push the elbows in a slow, steady manner in their first contests.

7.24 HANDSHAKE WRESTLING

Skill Level:
Peewee, junior high, senior high

Basic Skills:
N/A

Purpose:
To exhibit power and balance in a combative setting

Prerequisite:
None

Procedure: Wrestlers face each other, use a "shaking hands" grip, and place their right feet side by side. The object is to force the opponent to move either of his feet or to touch the mat with a hand or knee.

Coaching Points: This exercise is useful at the end of practice or as a physical education activity. Other grips, such as hand-on-elbow, could be used for this contest.

7.25 LEG WRESTLE

Skill Level:
Peewee, junior high, senior high

Basic Skills:
N/A

Purpose:
To have fun on a wrestling mat

Prerequisite:
None

Procedure: The wrestlers lie side by side with their heads pointing in opposite directions and their right elbows hooked. They raise their right legs three times, each time bumping their knees together. The third time, they hook their legs at the knee and attempt to force each other into a backward roll.

Coaching Points: Make sure that competing wrestlers are similar in weight.

7.26 CIRCLE GAMES

Skill Level:
Peewee, junior high, senior high

Basic Skills:
N/A

Purpose:
To develop balance and to have fun in a competitive setting

Prerequisite:
None

Procedure: All of these circle games are to be played by two wrestlers at a time in a 10-foot circle.

Cockfight.   Each wrestler holds a foot off of the mat with a hand and attempts to force the other out of the circle.

Ankle Grab.   Each wrestler bends over, grabs his own ankles, and then attempts to bump the other out of the circle.

Single Leg Bump.   Each wrestler raises his right leg off the mat, folds his arms in front of himself, and tries to force the other off of the mat using only the raised leg.

Coaching Points: These circle games can be used for combative contests at the end of wrestling practice or during a physical education wrestling unit.

7.27 KNEE FOOTBALL

Skill Level:
Junior high, senior high

Basic Skills:
N/A

Purpose:
To be used as an alternative to a regular wrestling practice

Prerequisite:
None

Procedure: This game is played in a wrestling room with the walls serving as the out-of-bounds lines. Goal lines are drawn with tape at both ends of the room. The wrestlers are divided into two teams, and rules are similar to regular football rules. A team has four downs to make a touchdown or first down. First downs are accomplished by completing two passes beyond the line of scrimmage. Teams may run only once every four downs. No participant may stand on his feet (this limits contact to low-impact wrestling-like contact). Teams must announce their intentions on the fourth down: punt or go for a score. The ball is thrown for kickoffs and punts. It is legal to catch balls off the walls. A regular football, nerf football, or taped towel may be used for the ball.

SAFETY CONCERNS
Insist that all action stop on the whistle, to cut down the chance of injury (even though the chance is minimal because most contact is low-impact). The smaller wrestlers will have a tendency to avoid piling up or going head up with the heavyweights.

7.28 SNAKE

Skill Level:
Peewee

Basic Skills:
N/A

Purpose:
To simulate the crawl position a wrestler might use to regain his base in the down position

Prerequisite:
None

Procedure: Wrestlers are instructed to stay within the confines of the large wrestling circle. One wrestler is designated as the snake; he slithers around on his belly attempting to tag the other wrestlers, who are running about on their feet. As a wrestler is tapped, he too becomes a snake. This continues until only one wrestler is left standing. He is declared the winner and will be the snake for the start of the next game.

Coaching Points: You may wish to modify this contest and play Squirrel instead, which is the same game except that wrestlers are allowed to move on their hands and knees instead of on their bellies.

7.29 DUCK DUCK GOOSE

Skill Level:
Peewee, junior high

Basic Skills:
N/A

Purpose:
To provide simple fun for elementary and middle school wrestlers on the wrestling mat

Prerequisite:
None

Procedure: All but one of the wrestlers sit Indian style in a circle; they are the ducks. The other wrestler is the goose and walks around the outside of the circle tapping the heads of the sitting wrestlers. Each time the goose taps a head he will say "Duck." To challenge a certain wrestler for his spot on the mat, he says "Goose." Immediately both wrestlers run around the circle to reach the vacated spot on the mat. If the duck can catch the goose and tap him, he gets to sit back in his spot. If the duck does not tap the goose, he becomes the goose for the next round.

Coaching Points: This should only be used for elementary or middle school children in a wrestling practice room or in a physical education setting.

7.30 THUMB WRESTLING

Skill Level:
Peewee

Basic Skills:
N/A

Purpose:
To develop fine motor skills and to get youngsters thinking about wrestling

Prerequisite:
None

Procedure: The opponents lock their right hands using a chin grip (fingers only). They then tap their thumbs together three times. The contest begins after the third tap. The object is to pin the thumb of the opponent to the top of the index finger, which serves as the mat. Instruct the combatants that to score a pin they must count "1,001, 1,002, . . . " and not "1-2-3" as in the media-pro wrestling.

Coaching Points: Children can imagine themselves as Greco-Roman wrestlers, going out to win with brute strength, or as slick-sters, baiting their opponents by laying their thumbs near a pin position only to duck out for a pin of their own at the last second. A "just for fun" activity.

7.31 KNOCK DOWN

Skill Level:
Peewee, junior high, senior high

Basic Skills:
N/A

Purpose:
To have fun on a wrestling mat and to provide a weight reduction workout

Prerequisite:
None

Procedure: The wrestlers are in a wrestling room with a Nerf soccer ball or Nerf volleyball. The object of the game is to "knock down" (hit) each of the other wrestlers in the room. The last man standing is the champion. The game begins with the coach throwing the ball into the air. The wrestler who catches the ball is allowed to take a maximum of three steps in trying to hit another wrestler with the ball. When a wrestler is hit, he must sit on his knees. If a wrestler catches the ball, then the person who threw the ball must sit down. A wrestler who has been "knocked down" may get back up if he gets the ball back. However, a downed man is not allowed to move around to get a loose ball; he must instead intercept a thrown or rolling ball.

Coaching Points: The wrestlers are constantly moving during this game, and it is a fun activity that can be used for losing weight. This game can be played in teams.

7.32 VISION QUEST

Skill Level:
Junior high, senior high

Basic Skills:
N/A

Purpose:
To be used for a "psych" session
before dual meets or tournaments

Prerequisite:
None

Procedure: All wrestlers on the team form a big circle and lie belly down. They pound on the mat and, if the coach desires, chant "Beat Smithfield" or whomever the next opponent happens to be. As the team pounds on the mat, one wrestler stands up and runs around the circle, stepping in between each wrestler. When he completes the circle and lies back down, the next wrestler beside him does the same thing. Each wrestler rounds the circle, and then the coach gives his goal-oriented psychological speech for the upcoming match.

Coaching Points: This exercise is mainly for ritual situations. It's of limited benefit for actual wrestling training or competition.

CHAPTER 8

WARM-UP, CONDITIONING, AND ENDURANCE ACTIVITIES

This chapter explores exercises that warm up the wrestler, build endurance, increase flexibility, and help maintain strength during the season.

Weight lifting is not discussed here because so many weight training books are currently on the market. However, most successful wrestling programs include weight training as part of the training regime.

This chapter begins with an explanation of the International Team Warm-up, which the Soviet Union team has shown to be effective. Next a preseason conditioning program used by Brandon High School in Florida is described. Coach Russ Cozart's teams have not lost a dual meet in almost 2 decades, and they begin every season with this 10-day conditioning camp. The chapter concludes with various conditioning exercises and routines that are being used by schools around the United States.

The exercises in this chapter can be valuable aids for the coach who wishes to add variety to his warm-ups and conditioning regime.

8.1 INTERNATIONAL TEAM WARM-UP

Skill Level:
Peewee, junior high, senior high, college

Basic Skills:
Position, motion, level change, penetration

Purpose:
To increase blood flow and elevate body temperature before stretching exercises and actual practice

Prerequisite:
None

Procedure: The captain leads the other wrestlers around the wrestling room in single file, jogging, the wrestlers mirroring the captain's movements. Many motor activities can be mixed in with the jogging, including penetration steps, two-leg hops, one-leg hops, skipping, cartwheels, somersaults, shoulder rolls, backward running, carioca, handsprings, headsprings, "walking like an egyptian," seal walks, hand–foot taps, and buddy-carries. This warm-up activity should take about 8 to 12 mintues.

Coaching Points: It is enjoyable to rotate leaders and have them come up with other creative motor activities. You may wish to play music or have the wrestlers sing as they exercise.

SAFETY CONCERNS
Do not select gymnastic stunts such as back flips or handsprings for any group that has not had prior experience in executing those types of skills.

8.2 THE BRANDON
10-DAY PRESEASON CONDITIONING CAMP

Skill Level:
Junior high, senior high, college

Purpose:
To improve cardiorespiratory function and the condition of various muscle groups essential for wrestling, to provide a symbol of physical excellence, and to give wrestlers a feeling of team unity

Basic Skills:
Position, motion, level change, penetration, lifting, back arch

Prerequisite:
The wrestlers should have participated in a basic weight training or conditioning program before beginning the 10-day program.

Procedure: The camp is held just before the beginning of the season, and all students in the school setting are encouraged to participate. It runs for 3 weeks, beginning on a Wednesday and continuing on the following schedule: Thursday, Monday, Tuesday, Wednesday, Thursday, Monday, Tuesday, and Wednesday, then ending with various competitions on Thursday (Day 10). No workouts are scheduled for Fridays or the weekends due to football season. All participants who complete every one of each day's scheduled exercises are presented with a T-shirt signifying their accomplishment. Participants who win the various contests are presented with wrestling memorabilia, such as wrestling posters or wrestling belt buckles.

The following paragraphs describe the basic daily workout and are followed by a chart that lists the entire 10-day cycle. The workout begins outside each day with the wrestlers doing three sets of pull-ups (maxing on each set), three sets of push-ups (maximum for 1-minute time period), and three sets of sit-ups (maximum for 1-minute time period). The wrestlers use three different grips for the pull-ups: palms away, palms forward, and baseball grip.

Next comes an isometric neck exercise. One man is in a position with one knee up and one knee down (Figure A). His partner lays his head on the knee that is up and straightens his body for a prescribed time period. All of his weight is supported by his neck and feet.

A

The wrestlers then do a timed run varying in distance from 1.4 to 3.5 miles and return to the wrestling room. Once the workout has moved indoors, the wrestlers complete a circuit training exercise routine consisting of neck work, handstand push-ups, buddys (inverted sit-ups), pummeling, lift drills, arching drills, jumping rope, climbing rope, and jump squats. Each wrestler goes through the circuit three times, and each time the amount of exercises to be performed changes. For instance, the inverted push-ups are done for 15 repetitions the first time, maxing to total fatigue the second time, and then 10 repetitions the third time. The times and amount also change over the 10-day period.

The following are brief explanations of each exercise.

Neck Work. The three neck exercises used in this circuit are the Bridge-Around–High Leg (Drill 6.16), Pullover Bridge with a partner (Drill 8.8), and bridging with a partner sitting on the thighs (Drill 8.9).

Buddys. The inverted sit-up is executed by the light wrestler lying flat on the mat in a belly-up position. He does the sit-ups after proper position has been attained. The dark wrestler steps between the light wrestler's legs, bends over, and locks around his own knees. He then picks the light wrestler up, forming a horizontal surface underneath the light wrestler's buttocks with his knees. The light wrestler is now in position for sit-ups (Figure B).

B

Handstand Push-Ups. A partner holds the legs for balance (Figure C).

C

Pummeling. (see Drill 2.3)

Lift Drills. (see Drill 2.1)

Arching Drills. The arching drills consist of bridging from the knees (sitting on the knees and leaning back into a back bridge), Hand-Walk the Wall back arch (Drill 2.7), walking on the hands (with help if needed), and the Hand Grip–Back Arch (Drill 2.9).

Jumping Rope. The wrestlers skip rope for a prescribed time period.

Climbing Rope. The wrestlers climb a rope (a) without using their legs, (b) using their legs, and (c) Donkey Kong style—two ropes at the same time, one arm on each rope.

Jump Squats. The wrestlers put their hands on their heads and repeatedly jump up in the air and down into a low squat position.

The daily workouts conclude with several sprints approximately the length of a gym. The coach evaluates the day's work while the wrestlers rest in squat positions, leaning against the wall. On Day 8 the wrestlers participate in a 2-mile buddy carry, carrying each other for a 2-mile timed distance run, switching roles whenever fatigue dictates. Day 9 includes a 3.5-mile timed run. Day 10 consists of a chin-up contest, a 6-mile timed run, and a softball game. The boys are divided into two teams for the Day 10 activities; usually it's varsity versus the new kids, with the winning team awarded fruit drinks and fruits immediately following the half-hour softball game.

Coaching Points: You might have participants get a physical examination before they start this workout. This is an excellent preseason conditioning routine because it not only stresses cardiovascular endurance but also begins toning muscles and includes muscle movements that will be needed for the upcoming wrestling season. The daily workouts last approximately 2 hours, and you should record all exercises requiring timing or a maximum output so you can pick out the champions in each event.

Day 1 Wednesday	Day 2 Thursday	Day 3 Monday	Day 4 Tuesday	Day 5 Wednesday
Max pulls 3× Max push-ups 3× Max sit-ups 3×	1 min per set	Same	Same	Same
Neck isometrics:30	:45	:45	1:00	1:00
Run 1.4	3 mi	Same	3.5 mi	1.4 fast
Neck 3 sets (1-5) 1) Flip spin 2) Kickover 3) Sit on thighs	Same	Same	Same	Same
Handstand push-ups 15/max 1 min/10	Same	2 set max/ 1 easy	2 max/1 hands touch	Max/max/10
Buddys 10/max 1 min/10	Same	2 set max/ 1 easy	2 max/use hands/fast	Max/max/10
Pummel :30/:30/100	45 30 45	1 min	1:15/45/120 count	1:00/100 count/ 1:15
Lifting 6 doubles/ single leg ducks	Fire 3×	3× double	3×/10 ea	15/6/12
Neck 6-10 bridge on knee/walk wall/ walk on hands/hand grip–back arch	Same	Same	Same	Same
Rope jump 1:15/:30/1:20	1:00/3×	3×/1:00	1:15 :30 1:20	1:00 :30 1:30
Ropes fast/no leg/Donkey Kong	3× Kong	All	All	All
Squat jumps 10–×3	11–3×	12 × 3	14-3 sets	15 × 3 sets
4 sprints and sit on wall/2 min	4-8 2:00	4-8 2:00	4-8 2:00	7-8 2:30

(Cont.)

203

	Day 6 Thursday	Day 7 Monday	Day 8 Tuesday	Day 9 Wednesday
Max pulls 3× Max push-ups 1 min per set Max sit-ups 3×		Same	Same	Same
Neck isometrics 1:15		1:30	1:45	2:00
Run 3 hard		3.5 mi	2-mi buddy carry	
Neck 3 sets (1-5) 1) Flip spin 2) Kickover 3) Sit on thighs		Same	Same	Same
Handstand push-ups Max/max/hands touch		Max/20/18	Max/max/hands together	
Buddys Max/max/use		Max/15/10	Max/max/hands behind head	Same
Pummel 1:30/1:15/100 count		1:30/100 count/ 1:15	1:45/100 count/ 1:30	Same
Lifting 12/10/8		Same	Same	Same
Neck 6-10 bridge on knee/walk wall/ walk on hands/hand grip-back arch		Same	Same	Same
Rope jump 1:00/:30 fast/2:00		1:30 :45 fast 2:00	1:30 :45 fast 2:00	2:00 :45 2:00
Ropes 3× Kong		All	All	All
Squat jumps 16 × 3 sets		17 × 3 sets	18 × 3	19 × 3
8-9 sprints and sit on wall/2:30		4-8 3:00	4-8 3:00	4-8 3:00

Day 10 Thursday

Teams:

Chin-up contest
6-mi run
Baseball game

To Classroom:

1) Shirt presentations
2) Winning Team: Fruit, fruit juice
3) Mr. Exercise Award

8.3 THE READY SANDBAG WORKOUT

Skill Level:
Junior high, senior high, college

Basic Skills:
N/A

Purpose:
To provide a cardiovascular workout with equal muscular-endurance and strength-maintenance benefits

Prerequisite:
None

Procedure: This drill is known as a 12-by-12 workout. There are 12 exercises, and each is to be performed for 12 repetitions. Following completion of an exercise, a wrestler moves immediately to the next exercise without resting, thus allowing for a positive cardiovascular effect.

Back Bridge. The wrestler gets into a back bridge and holds the sandbag on his chest, pressing it until his arms are completely extended. The motion is similar to a bench press (Figure A).

A

Hack Squat. The wrestler stands, holding the sandbag between his legs. He grasps the bag with one hand in front of his legs and one hand behind his legs, then performs regular squats (Figure B).

B

Triceps Extension. The wrestler holds the bag behind his head while in a standing position. He presses the bag in a manner similar to a french curl (Figure C).

C

Regular Squat.   The wrestler holds the bag on his shoulder and performs regular squats.

Upright Row.   The wrestler spreads his legs and bends over, forming a 120-degree angle at the waist, keeping his back parallel to the floor, and then lifts the bag to his chest 12 times.

Back Squats.   The wrestler holds the bag behind his buttocks and completes 12 squats.

Zimmers.   The wrestler does jump squats while holding the bag to his chest.

Bent Rows.   This is the same as upright rows except the wrestler is bent over to a 90-degree angle at the waist.

Calf Raises.   The wrestler holds the bag on his shoulders and raises up on his toes for 12 repetitions.

Front Press.   This is a regular military press using the bag and pressing it overhead for 12 repetitions.

Behind Head Press.   This is a military press, but holding the bag behind the head for 12 repetitions.

Biceps Curls.   This exercise consists of curling the sandbag for 12 repetitions.

Coaching Points: This routine is very beneficial as a total body workout. It affects almost every muscle group in the body and promotes cardiovascular development. The routine can be completed in a very short period of time. Use differently weighted bags for the various weight classes. For example, use 25-pound bags for lightweights, 35-pound bags for middleweights, and 45-pound bags for heavyweights.

SAFETY CONCERNS

If sandbags are used at the junior high level, make sure wrestlers have been instructed in basic weight training principles and movements.

8.4 PTA (PAIN, TORTURE, AGONY)*

Skill Level:
Junior high, senior high, college

Purpose:
To engage in a series of high-intensity wrestling-related activities to push beyond the normal range of mental and physical fatigue, thus allowing for maximum physical performance in a competitive setting

Basic Skills:
Position, motion, level change, penetration, backstep, back arch, (subskills—hand control, chaining)

Prerequisite:
The wrestlers must be able to perform basic wrestling exercises and maneuvers.

Procedure: The wrestlers are instructed that they will engage in a series of physical activities involving constant motion for a given time period, usually 8 to 15 minutes. They are informed that no matter how tired they may feel, their bodies have the physical ability to continue to perform. (The PTA routine is a mind-over-matter exercise designed to develop mental toughness.)

Because these routines include numerous buddy exercises, wrestlers should choose partners. A coach may incorporate any activity into the PTA routine and should vary the activities depending upon the effects desired. Listed here are two samples of 10-minute PTA routines; the first incorporates mostly wrestling skills, and the second is designed specifically for physical endurance.

Routine 1
Wrestling Skill PTA
1. Snaps and spins
   (see Drill 5.5)
2. Snap-spin and Butt drag
   (see Drills 4.9 & 5.5)
3. Floating
   (see Drill 5.6)
4. Shoot and Leap frog
   (see Drill 8.15)

Routine 2
Physical Endurance PTA
1. Run in place
2. Hop to ceiling
3. Wheelbarrow push-ups
4. Grass drills
5. Sit-out and roll-even
6. Buddy carries around room

---

*This routine was designed by Neil Turner at Lock Haven University and is used extensively in the Lock Haven Summer Wrestling Training Program, which trains over 1,900 scholastic wrestlers each summer. For more information, contact Neil Turner, Head Wrestling Coach, Lock Haven University, Lock Haven, Pennsylvania 17745.

5. Penetration shots (solo)
   (see Drill 1.11)

6. Double-ups
   (see Drill 1.26)

7. Run in place and sprawl
   (sprawl on whistle)

8. Pummel
   (see Drill 2.3)

9. Spinning
   (see Drill 5.1)

10. Body lifts
    (see Drill 2.1)

7. Push-ups

8. Buddy hops
   (hop over partner in referee's position)

9. Buddy squats

10. Squat thrusts

Note: Unless otherwise stated, each wrestler performs the exercise for 30 seconds.

Coaching Points: You might want to combine activities from each routine to form a third routine to emphasize the performance of simple wrestling skills while the wrestler's bodies are fatigued. To obtain maximum physical benefits, the PTA routine should be held toward the end of practice so that the wrestlers' heart rates will already be elevated.

8.5 MAT PULL-UPS

Skill Level:
Junior high, senior high, college

Basic Skills:
N/A

Purpose:
This exercise allows wrestlers to do pull-ups even when no pull-up bar is available in the wrestling room

Prerequisite:
None

Procedure: One wrestler lies flat on his back with a partner standing over him straddling his chest area. The wrestler standing lets his arms hang to his sides, raising only his forearms to form a 90-degree angle at the elbows. The down man reaches up and holds on to the standing man's wrists. He must maintain a rigid position to do mat pull-ups; only his heels will be on the mat.

Coaching Points: Not only is this an excellent conditioning exercise for the down wrestler, but it also offers an isometric contraction for the arms of the standing man.

8.6 TOWEL PULL-UPS

Skill Level:
Peewee, junior high, senior high, college

Purpose:
To increase a wrestler's grip while developing the "pull" muscles needed for capturing a single leg

Basic Skills:
N/A

Prerequisite:
None

Procedure: A towel should be thrown over a pull-up bar. Wrestlers execute their pull-ups while grasping each end of the hanging towel instead of using the pull-up bar.

Coaching Points: This exercise not only increases a wrestler's grip but also more exactly duplicates a single leg attack. Encourage this type of pull-up exercise because of the multiple benefits attained.

8.7 TWO-MAN SIT-UPS

Skill Level:
Junior high, senior high, college

Basic Skills:
N/A

Purpose:
To add flexibility to the sit-up motion and allow a wrestler to exercise muscles past the normal range of motion of a regular sit-up

Prerequisite:
None

Procedure: One wrestler assumes a down referee's position and his partner sits on his back. The top man faces toward the buttocks of the bottom man and hooks his feet in the bottom man's thigh region. He is now ready to do sit-ups, attempting to touch his head on or near the mat with each repetition. If needed, the bottom man may use his neck to aid the top man in coming back into the upright position.

Coaching Points: You may want your wrestlers to turn belly-down in the same position and perform back hyperextension immediately following the sit-up exercise to strengthen the back muscles.

8.8 PULLOVER BRIDGE

Skill Level:
Junior high, senior high, college

Basic Skills:
N/A

Purpose:
To strengthen the neck muscles while in a bridge position and to execute movement

Prerequisite:
None

A

B

C

Procedure: The dark wrestler assumes a back bridge, extending his arms and grasping the ankles of his partner, who is standing in front of him. The dark wrestler kicks over into a front bridge with his legs to the side of his partner. The dark wrestler then kicks back into the back bridge position. The bridging wrestler should kick into his front bridge on both sides of his partner and finally kick straight over so that he straddles his partner's legs (Figures A, B, C).

Coaching Points: The wrestlers will have to pull with their arms to make this drill work at first. This drill can also be performed by two wrestlers both in back bridges, grasping hands in a head-to-head position (Figure D).

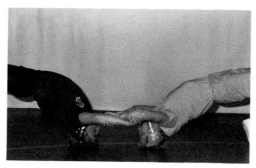

D

8.9 TWO-MAN BRIDGE

Skill Level:
Senior high, college

Basic Skills:
N/A

Purpose:
To condition neck muscles that are needed for bridging when attempting to avoid a pinning situation

Prerequisite:
The wrestlers should be able to bridge by themselves.

A

B

Procedure: One wrestler lies on his back and moves into a back bridge position. His partner lies across his chest to provide added resistance (Figure A). After the wrestlers have become accustomed to this type of exercise, the top man sits on the bridging wrestler's thighs, placing his feet on his chest (Figure B). This offers added resistance.

Coaching Points: This drill can be expanded to include a live combat scenario, in which the top wrestler applies a half nelson–crotch combination. The bottom wrestler, on the coach's signal, attempts to bridge and escape from the pinning situation.

SAFETY CONCERNS
You must be cautious about using this exercise for younger wrestlers, due to their physical immaturity. It does provide an excellent match-like situation for the older boys who have full physical development.

8.10 BACK PULLOVERS

Skill Level:
Junior high, senior high, college

Basic Skills:
N/A

Purpose:
To increase flexibility of the back muscles and to experience kinesthetic awareness of being thrown

Prerequisite:
None

A

B

C

Procedure: Two wrestlers stand up back to back, extend their arms over their heads, and grasp hands using a finger-chain grip (Figure A). One wrestler bends forward, pulling his partner over his back into a standing position (Figures B, C).

Coaching Points: This drill should be performed before using back arch maneuvers.

8.11 HEAD LIFT DRILL

Skill Level:
Senior high, college

Basic Skill:
Lifting

Purpose:
To lift an opponent from the mat using only the head for support

Prerequisite:
The wrestlers should have performed numerous neck-strengthening and flexibility exercises.

Procedure: The dark wrestler assumes a one-knee-up, one-knee-down position; the light wrestler leans over dark's head. On command, the dark wrestler comes to his feet, lifting light into the air, using only his head for support and balance.

Coaching Points: Inform the wrestlers that in certain situations they will have to use their heads to lift or drive an opponent.

SAFETY CONCERNS
Wrestlers should perform exercise routines designed to strengthen the neck muscles before attempting this type of lift. In any case, make sure that the wrestlers have completed flexibility exercises before attempting this skill.

8.12 BODY CURL

Skill Level:
Senior high, college

Basic Skills:
Back arch, (subskill—hip thurst)

Purpose:
To allow wrestlers to execute a curling-type exercise without using a barbell or weights, and to work on a basic hip thrust, which is an important skill for lifting or arching

Prerequisite:
The wrestlers should be able to curl using a barbell.

Procedure: One wrestler stands and his partner jumps into his arms as if he were a baby. The wrestler holding the "baby" then uses his arms to curl the body. If the partner is too heavy to do a perfect curl, allow the wrestler to "cheat with his hips." The cheating motion creates a hip thrust; this skill is helpful for lifting, arching, and blocking penetration shots. However, if hip power is not desired, don't allow the wrestlers to cheat with their hips.

Coaching Points: You must realize that to develop maximum strength in the biceps area, the hips should not be used. However, hip power and movement are integral parts of wrestling, so the hip thrust provides some positive benefits.

8.13 BODY ROW

Skill Level:
Senior high, college

Basic Skills:
N/A

Purpose:
To be used as a rowing exercise when weights are not available

Prerequisite:
None

Procedure: The wrestlers start in a standing belly-to-back position with one wrestler attaining a rear standing bodylock position. The rear man lifts his partner from the mat and lowers him between his legs. The partner must maintain a perfectly rigid position (in other words, he must keep his body straight). After the rear man has lowered his partner between his legs, he lifts him back to a standing position. The next time he bends over, lowering his partner to the side, returns to the upright position, and finally lowers his partner to the other side. This routine should be repeated several times.

Coaching Points: This is an excellent exercise for developing lower back muscles. It is also an excellent exercise for training individuals for freestyle and Greco-Roman wrestling techniques, because some of those situations dictate lifting a wrestler from the mat.

8.14 MONKEY ROLL CONTEST

Skill Level:
Junior high, senior high

Basic Skills:
N/A

Purpose:
To enhance a wrestler's ability to scramble on the mat

Prerequisite:
None

Procedure: Three wrestlers lie belly-down. The wrestler on the right jumps over the middle wrestler, hits belly-down, and rolls under the wrestler on the left. The middle wrestler rolls to the right and repeats the same steps. The wrestler on the left has hopped over the first wrestler and rolled under the second wrestler, and now he stands and begins the same routine. The contest is to see how many times the first wrestler goes completely through the cycle.

Coaching Points: The monkey rolls can also be used as an agility drill for everyday practice.

8.15 SHOOT AND LEAP FROG

Skill Level:
Junior high, senior high, college

Purpose:
To be part of a circuit training exercise and used as a penetration drill

Basic Skills:
Level change, penetration

Prerequisite:
The wrestlers must be able to execute penetration.

A   B

Procedure: One wrestler simulates a low single penetration as he shoots between his partner's legs (Figure A). Immediately following his shot, he stands and leaps back over his partner's back (Figure B). The entire routine continues for a certain time period. Roles are reversed for the next time session.

Coaching Points: Be careful that the low single shots do not become an "overextended dive through." The overextension is a bad habit that may carry over into a match situation. Overextension during penetration may allow an opponent to score a takedown using a snapdown maneuver. This drill is also known as going "in and out of the window."

8.16 PARTNER DIVE-OVERS

Skill Level:
Peewee, junior high, senior high

Basic Skills:
N/A

Purpose:
To increase flexibility of the muscles in the lower back area

Prerequisite:
None

Procedure: One wrestler assumes a down referee's position. His partner stands beside him, bends over, and grasps onto his neck and stomach area. He then executes a forward roll, maintaining his grip so that he ends up in a back arch position with his head under his partner's stomach. He then kicks back into the starting position and repeats the exercise.

Coaching Points: The bottom man must assume a sturdy base for the exercise to be successful.

8.17 HAND GRIP

Skill Level:
Junior high, senior high, college

Basic Skills:
N/A

Purpose:
To develop a strong hand grip

Prerequisite:
None

Procedure: A wrestler can increase the strength of his hand grip by squeezing a tennis ball or a piece of the mat. Pieces of scrap mat can be cut to fit a wrestler's hand and can be carried in a jacket pocket. The wrestler should squeeze the ball or mat for at least 10 seconds per repetition. Unlimited repetitions may be performed.

Coaching Points: This is an exercise wrestlers can perform on the bus, at lunchtime, or just walking down the hall at school.

ABOUT THE
AUTHOR

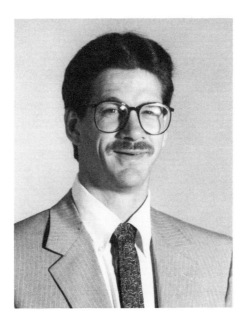

Dennis Johnson is a USA Wrestling Bronze Level–Certified coach who has coached high school wrestling since 1976. In addition, he has worked as a clinician in camp settings and directs his own camp in Warren, Pennsylvania. Johnson has studied wrestling in the Soviet Union at Moscow's Institute of Sport and Physical Education. He has also authored several articles on wrestling technique for *Scholastic Coach* magazine.

Johnson is a member of USA Wrestling, The National Wrestling Coaches Association, and the Pennsylvania Wrestling Coaches Association. He is a physical education instructor and wrestling coach in Warren County, Pennsylvania.